HISTORIC REDWOOD
NATIONAL AND STATE PARKS

Also by Gail L. Jenner

Ankle High and Knee Deep: Women Reflect on Western Rural Life
Western Siskiyou County: Gold & Dreams
Images of the State of Jefferson
The State of Jefferson: Then & Now
Postcards from the State of Jefferson
Historic Inns and Eateries in the State of Jefferson
Across the Sweet Grass Hills, Winner of the 2002 WILLA Literary
 Award
Black Bart: The Poet Bandit

HISTORIC REDWOOD
NATIONAL AND STATE PARKS

The Stories Behind One of America's Great Treasures

GAIL L. JENNER

Guilford, Connecticut

An imprint of Rowman & Littlefield

Distributed by NATIONAL BOOK NETWORK

British Library Cataloguing in Publication Information Available

Library of Congress Cataloging-in-Publication Data is available on file.

ISBN 978-1-4930-1809-3 (paperback)
ISBN 978-1-4930-1810-9 (e-book)

♾™ The paper used in this publication meets the minimum requirements of American National Standard for Information Sciences—Permanence of Paper for Printed Library Materials, ANSI/NISO Z39.48-1992.

Contents

INTRODUCTION

As one travels US Highway 101, what was once called the Redwood Highway, it's easy to overlook the real impact of the redwoods. Yes, many people stop and stare up at a few of the taller, more impressive trees along the highway. Or, maybe they'll take one of the loops through the trees and marvel at them—for a few miles anyway—and hug a tree or two as they snap photos on their phones or cameras.

But, when you truly get off the beaten track and immerse yourself in the deep shade and overwhelmingly peaceful and stunning world found within, under, and around the Tall Trees, it takes your breath away. In the silence you have to sigh and inhale deeply; even the scent of the trees and abounding undergrowth awakens the deepest part of your nature. Finally you begin to sense the otherworldly character of these ancient, massive trees. They speak of *time*—and the passage of time. Some are six hundred years old; some are a thousand years old. A few are, perhaps, two thousand years old. Some stand over 350 feet tall, with a girth of 15 or 20 feet. Whatever their height or breadth, however, they are magnificent. They are awe-inspiring, and they speak of a past cloaked in mystery and rich history.

Such is the captivating world found within and around the Redwood National and State Parks (RNSP) located in the far northwestern corner of California. A federal park, the four parks that make up the Redwood National and State Parks fall under the jurisdiction of the National Park Service (NPS) while cooperatively managed by NPS and the California Department of Parks and Recreation (CDPR).

This breathtaking world is a unique one and the parks' eventual designation was won only after much controversy and debate. Those who pursued protection of the great trees persevered despite great challenges.

After the initial purchase of 166 acres, which became Prairie Creek Redwoods State Park in 1923, and the eventual creation of Redwood National Park in 1968, conservationists as well as a concerned public have continued to push for greater protection of California's redwoods. Moreover, today the National Park Service's goal of preservation is linked to its secondary, long-range goal of restoration. As noted in the parks' General Management Plan/General Plan (2000), "[the ultimate goal] is to restore and maintain the RNSP ecosystems as they would have evolved without human influences since 1850 and perpetuate ongoing natural processes."

In truth, however, the physical history of the region is linked to the history of the various and distinct human populations that have interacted with it, from pre-contact times to the present. This impact has left its indelible imprint on the land and the environment, and to appreciate the story of the Redwood National and State Parks' evolution and creation, it is important to look at the scope of human history, as well.

There are few words that can adequately describe what the redwoods mean to the people who have spent generations living as part of them. Taking a step backwards in time to when the original people of the forests lived within the redwood coastal belt reveals just how connected their lives were to the environment they occupy. Their lives were—and are—built on more than just the wood, although the redwood was the source of much of their material culture; their lives were enmeshed in the very character and fabric of the trees.

The trees lived and breathed life into them. As Minni Reeves, Chilula tribal elder and religious leader, Hupa Indian Reservation, said in an interview in 1976, the Chilula are the "people from *within* the redwood tree." To the Yurok, redwood trees are living beings that stand as "guardians" over sacred places.

Finally, according to Edwin C. Bearss in *Redwood National Park: History/Basic Data*, a house, to the coastal tribes, "was understood to be a living being. The redwood that formed its planks was itself the body of one of the Spirit Beings. Spirit Beings were believed to be a divine race who existed before humans in the redwood region and who taught people the proper way to live here." Even those who spent their lives in the forest as woodsmen and loggers found a source of strength deep within these dense forests—not comprehending, perhaps, the scope of their destruction, but loving the trees all the same.

Though redwood forests originally covered up to two million acres, Redwood National Park—along with three California State Redwood Parks, including Del Norte Coast Redwoods State Park, Jedediah Smith Redwoods State Park, and Prairie Creek Redwoods State Park—currently protect 131,983 acres (federal: 71,715; state: 60,268). And because more than 90 percent of the redwoods that once ranged from above the Oregon border down to the central California coastline are gone now, Redwood National and State Parks is even more important than as just a tourist destination.

E. C. Williams, one of the first men to pursue the commercial value of redwood, reminisced in 1912 about his first journey through the redwood wilderness in the spring of 1850. He remarked that the groves of redwoods were, in fact, "God's first temples," as declared in Bryant's *Thanatopsis.*

In retrospect, Williams also wrote, "I cannot but regret the part it appeared necessary for me to enact in what now looks like a desecration." Perhaps, with hindsight being 20/20, we recognize how seriously we must take the preservation of the redwoods. It is not just for the present we protect the redwoods, nor is it just to preserve the past—it is for the future. The future of mankind . . .

As Minni Reeves so elegantly explained: "The redwood trees have a lot of power: they are the tallest, live the longest, and are the most beautiful trees in the world. Destroy these trees and you destroy the Creator's love. And if you destroy that which the Creator loves so much, you will eventually destroy mankind."

Acknowledgments

IN PUTTING TOGETHER THIS BOOK, IT SEEMED IMPOSSIBLE TO SEPARATE the Redwood National and State Parks' history from the general history of the Tall Trees through time: how they evolved, how the first people interacted with them, how the environment as well as the corresponding flora and fauna relied on them, how industries grew up dependent upon them, and how those who recognized their importance worked to preserve them. These smaller "chapters" seem to pre-date the actual history of the movement to create the Redwood National and State Parks and thus, I am including them in this history as well.

Any research project depends on many people, making it impossible to acknowledge them all—especially the librarians and museum curators who helped me as I poked and plodded through the initial days of this journey "into the redwoods." I spoke with a number of people in my travels and in my search. I owe them all many thanks. With regard to the material and research related to the history behind the creation of Redwood National and State Park, however, I'd especially like to thank James B. Wheeler, NPS Ranger/interpreter in Orick, who provided me with information and materials, answered a number of questions, and offered critical suggestions.

I'd like to thank Robert McConnell, Yurok archaeological field coordinator, who granted me an interview and shared stories and materials of the Yurok people. I'd also like to thank Mike Kellogg of the Timber Heritage Association, who took me on a tour (and for a ride on a railroad car) and shared the history and artifacts that he and the association are working hard to preserve. I hope their dream of a museum will come to fruition. It's an important aspect of the history of the redwoods.

And I'd like to thank Dr. Sari Sommarstrom, who has worked as a consultant on natural resource planning, watershed management, and restoration projects for many years and who generously provided me with materials on the region.

I must thank my family, too, for the time they spent reading and rereading my material, asking me questions, finding books and photos, and—through it all—kindly allowing me to spend the hours and weeks necessary to put my research together.

Lastly, I would like to thank my editor, Mike Urban, for asking me to take on this project. It's been a challenging but rewarding journey.

Those Amazing Redwoods:
How They Came to Be

The redwoods, once seen, leave a mark or create a vision that stays with you always. No one has ever successfully painted or photographed a redwood tree. The feeling they produce is not transferable. From them comes silence and awe. It's not only their unbelievable stature, nor the color which seems to shift and vary under your eyes, no, they are not like any trees we know, they are ambassadors from another time.
—JOHN STEINBECK, *TRAVELS WITH CHARLEY: IN SEARCH OF AMERICA*

WHEN ONE ENTERS A STAND OF THE IMMENSE TREES WE CALL RED-woods, or *Sequoia sempervirens* (meaning "ever living"), it's almost impossible to comprehend how much land these magnificent trees once covered or how they came to be. They actually descend from ancient times and provide a living link to prehistory. Fossilized redwood has even been found in the deserts of Arizona.

Knowing their near-relatives were present during the age of dinosaurs, it's not hard to imagine a *Tyrannosaurus rex* tramping through a mist-shrouded forest looking for something to devour. The three-hundred-plus-foot redwoods stand like sentinels, their deep understory an ethereal world of greens and browns, shadows and light. As John C. Merriam, president of the Save-the-Redwoods League from 1921 to 1944 wrote, "While, through contrasts of their seemingly fantastic architecture, ancient castles may tell us of other ages, living trees like these connect us as by hand-touch with all the centuries they have known."

Sun breaks through the dense redwood forest.
FRANK PATTERSON, PHOTOGRAPHER

Ferdinand Lee Clark, who led a distinguished career in military as well as civilian life and was another early proponent of a state redwood park, wrote, "When these great trees were seedlings—the Egyptian Pyramids were fresh from the builders' hands—the foundation stones of those of South America were not yet laid. In those dim, distant days the very land from which they sprang was—geologists affirm—yet newly upheaved from the ocean depths" (Taylor, A. A. *California Redwood Park,* 1912).

Though the redwoods originally stretched from north of the Monterey County line to just over the Oregon border, today those groves have been significantly reduced as a result of decades of logging and land development.

The coastal redwood is cousin to the sequoias of central California and the dawn redwood of China. These majestic, mammoth trees now protected by the Redwood National and State Parks are distinctly different and unique, however, and a fragmented remnant of an ecosystem that once spanned the globe.

There are simply no other trees like the coast redwoods.

Paleobotanists believe that the ancestors of the coastal redwood developed during the Cretaceous period, 135 to 65 million years ago. The climate during this time was stable, more humid, and warmer than today. Very likely the trees spread during the Paleocene period, 65 to 24 million years ago, and eventually covered a broad sweep of territory worldwide. Then, slowly, as the climate changed and became cooler and drier, especially in northern Europe, the species retreated. By the end of the Tertiary period, three million years ago, the redwood vanished from Europe, Asia, Greenland, and Japan. This dramatic change in the world's climate meant that California's rugged coastal Mediterranean climate became the prime geographic location for the redwood. From the San Francisco Bay north, the cool Pacific weather, coupled with summertime fog, supports this remnant of the world's tallest trees, which, according to some estimates, once spanned nearly two million acres. The coast redwood is perfectly adapted to the region's unique environment, and its habitat includes forests, prairies, oak woodlands, and coastal marine environments.

Part of what makes the coastal redwoods in and around the Redwood National and State Parks (which is composed of Redwood National Park and three state parks) unique is what is required for them to grow. Amazingly, a redwood cone is about the size of an olive and contains anywhere from 60 to 120 seeds. It would take more than 100,000 seeds to weigh a pound. While one tree can drop 10 million seeds, only a few will mature,

3

but if one lands in the right environment, it may grow into one of the giants we see today, some being more than 2,000 years old.

Tracing the age of a redwood tells its own personal story. Because of its growth rings, in addition to its size and dimension, a coast redwood provides a relatively detailed map of history. More fascinating than a textbook!

In 1934 Professor Emmanuel Fritz, of the University of California, studied a fallen redwood in Richardson Grove State Park, located in Humboldt County. The tree fell in 1933 after its roots, damaged by fire earlier in its life, could not hold up the one-million-pound tree any longer. After the trunk was sawn through, Fritz was able to trace a series of events in the tree's 1,204-year life. The original ground level of the tree—estimated to have taken root circa 700 AD—was actually eleven feet below the surface of the soil when the tree fell.

The professor detailed these major events: The tree had survived at least nine fires, the first one in 1147 and again in 1595, 1789, and 1806; another close call with fire occurred in 1820 when the bark and cambium layers were burnt through, which literally "killed" about 40 percent of the tree's circumference. The tree had also experienced seven major floods in a thousand years.

If we look at a map of the Northern Hemisphere, it's easy to identify the temperate rain forest that stretches from Alaska to California, a rain forest exceedingly rich in tree species. The redwood is actually one of more than six hundred conifer species found around the world, a member of the Taxodiaceae family—large, fast-growing, and long-lived trees, with small seed cones. Uniquely, the coast redwood can sprout vertical shoots—even as many as a hundred or more—from its lateral roots located just under the soil's surface. It can also sprout new shoots from an old stump or burned-out tree.

The branches of a coast redwood often begin a hundred feet or more above the forest floor. The leaves are of two types: main shoots that have a spiral arrangement of needles, and short branchlets, which decrease in size near the tip. Some of these branchlets develop cones, approximately one-half to one inch long. Besides the redwood, the Douglas fir, grand fir, Port Orford cedar, Sitka spruce, western hemlock, and western red cedar populate the Northwest and coastal forests. Redwood National and State Parks harbors the tallest known Sitka spruce as well as the tallest redwoods. Many of the largest trees are found along the streams and rivers that drain the northern Coast Range and Klamath mountain range.

Four of California's northern counties—Del Norte, Humboldt, Mendocino, and Sonoma—are home to 88 percent of the surviving coastal redwoods. Though redwood forests once covered over two million acres, today Redwood National Park, in conjunction with three California state redwood parks—Del Norte Coast Redwoods State Park, Jedediah Smith Redwoods State Park, and Prairie Creek Redwoods State Park—currently protect 131,983 acres (federal: 71,715; state: 60,268). Out of that, old growth forest acreage totals 38,982 acres (federal: 19,640; state: 19,342).

Two distinct physical regions characterize the park: the coast and the mountains. The coastline is typically rugged and rocky and difficult to travel on foot, although there are some grassy and/or brushy slopes. Around Crescent City, there are broad flat beaches. Broad alluvial valleys spread out from the mouths of the Klamath River and Redwood Creek.

Much of northern California's coastline is characterized by rugged, rocky cliffs.
FRANK PATTERSON, PHOTOGRAPHER

At Prairie Creek Redwoods State Park, an eight-mile stretch of beach lies at the base of the one-hundred- to four-hundred-foot vertical Gold Bluffs, known as Gold Bluffs Beach.

The park's elevation rises from sea level to over three thousand feet; the steep slopes of the park, averaging 40 percent to 70 percent, are thus susceptible to erosion.

Interestingly, for forty years, from 1859 to 1899, there was one homestead located between Gold Bluffs and the mouth of the Klamath River: the Johnstons'. The site was known to travelers after Anthony and Julia Johnston settled the property in 1851. The Johnstons raised cattle on what became a 1,000-acre ranch, as well as mined for gold, and travelers knew they could always find a place to board. Their home was set a half-mile up on the bluffs above the ocean's shoreline.

Originally the trail that connected Crescent City and Humboldt Bay passed along the beach below the Johnstons' homestead. Traversing the bluffs meant, however, that travelers often had to hang onto their horses' tails as they climbed the steep bluffs. The trail was treacherous, and the waves crashing onto the shoreline were equally risky. Sadly, in 1891, Johnston's two sons were on the beach when a rogue wave caught them, throwing them against the bluffs. One son survived; the other was washed out to sea.

Eventually the county completed a wagon road that passed along the ridge rather than along the shore and up the bluffs.

In addition to geography, weather and rainfall create the moist, cool habitat redwoods require. They do not tolerate much snow or frost, nor can they survive harsh or long cold seasons. Coastal temperatures range between forty and sixty degrees Fahrenheit year-round, while inland winters are colder and summer temperatures hotter and drier. Although redwoods can be made to grow in a variety of environments, the giant redwoods need a specific habitat and are thus found in a 250-mile-long north–south belt that stretches from 1 to 2 miles offshore to not more than 50 miles inland. Here the trees are protected from heavy salt air while thriving on the fingers of fog that creep in and along the coast almost daily.

Ernest Ingersoll, in the January 1883 issue of *Harper's*, described the fog as being "held in the pockets of shade under the matted twigs and needles, and fall in misty showers, constantly refreshing the soil. Thus it happens that the redwood forests are particularly rich in a great variety of other trees and bushes; and a perfect jungle of undergrowth, shrub-like and herbaceous, flourishes there."

The three-hundred-foot giants actually draw in moisture from the fog through their uppermost needles, where the tree's normal circulation system doesn't reach, even as it miraculously transports four hundred gallons of water a day up its massive trunk from its shallow but extensive root system. In other words, redwoods create their own "rain" by trapping fog on their leaves, which then condenses into water droplets. And some of this rain also falls to the ground below, providing moisture for the plants living on the forest understory.

California's coastal region receives, on average, 60 to 100 inches of precipitation each year, almost all of it from October to April, but it can receive up to 122 inches of rain per year. A large redwood tree actually holds about 34,000 pounds of water. Fog can even alleviate the effects of drought because of the increased humidity, and since fog occurs more frequently during the dryer summer months, it is imperative that the redwood absorbs the moisture locked in fog.

Obviously redwoods thrive in the coastal fog belt and actually create their own "microclimate" because of it. Through transpiration, each tree can release five hundred gallons of water into the air daily. Residents along the California coastline call the weather created by the redwoods "natural air-conditioning."

Interestingly, when a redwood suffers from a lack of moisture, or moisture "stress," even the tallest trees can exhibit the results: Such trees might be dead at the highest points but be green and healthy below. Such trees are often called "spike-tops."

It's been estimated that fog provides at least 30 percent of the total amount of water a redwood requires. Unfortunately in areas where fewer redwoods are found—or where logging has occurred—there is a corresponding drop in the amount of moisture available to the trees. Areas of clear-cut receive significant amounts of solar radiation and have higher evaporation rates.

As noted by a reporter for the *San Francisco Call* in November 1895: "Lying within the fog belt on the west side of the Coast Range, never further than twenty miles from the coast, the gigantic redwoods breast the gales of the Pacific as though in derision of their even more gigantic brethren, the *Sequoia gigantea*, who choose the warm breezes and genial sunshine of the western Sierra foothills in the interior."

To say that the redwood is unique in the plant kingdom is an understatement. Quite clearly, the coast redwood has survived the eons because of its unique and hardy character, which ensures its ability to grow for hundreds, even thousands, of years as well as withstand attack or potential destruction. In a sense, it has many "tricks" to protect itself from disastrous events or other kinds of pervasive damage.

The bark of the tree is thick, up to a foot in some places. The chemical composition of the tree, which contains a tannic acid, makes it distasteful or even poisonous to pests, such as termites and ants. This is precisely why it is used in construction, because it can resist attack by carpenter ants and/or termites. Due to the absence of resin in its bark, it can also withstand fire, and even after successive fires will continue to grow. Fire as a tool of nature actually helps limit the amount of heavy undergrowth and provides open areas where younger saplings can stretch and grow; it also converts the abundant undergrowth into fertilizing ash. Finally, it kills off invading and destructive insect infestations.

The redwood is classified as softwood; it has a straight grain and is lightweight. The heartwood is the most valuable, and because it splits easily, much of the long clear timber in the early days was split into rails and posts. In fact, old growth trees were often earmarked for cutting into rails and other kinds of stakes and posts. As noted by G. F. Beranek in *High Climbers and Timber Fallers*, "A fine old growth redwood can yield volumes of clear heartwood that is absent of sapwood, coarse grain, knots and rot-qualities that second growth can't come close to matching."

The coast redwood is also monoecious, meaning it carries both male and female reproductive parts locked away in its cones. As noted, a single redwood cone, which is about the size of an olive, contains anywhere from 60 to 120 seeds. While seeds are shed from September until early summer, most are shed from November to February. Unfortunately only about 5 to 10 percent are viable. The others may be incomplete embryos or empty or deposited in environments not conducive to survival.

Uniquely, redwoods can also sprout from dormant buds or even from the trunk of a fallen or dying tree. If a live redwood falls to the ground, its limbs will be forced to begin growing. As a result, a "ring" of trees will grow up. These are often referred to as a cathedral or family grouping and are, in fact, genetic clones of each other.

Sometimes a ring of trees will also surround a fire-scarred stump, again creating a family circle. The normally dormant buds located at the base of the crippled tree germinate and begin to grow. This ability to sprout under various forms of stress insures the species' survival, for buds can appear even a hundred feet or more up on the trunk.

Redwood burls also provide another source of regrowth. A burl is a "lumpy" outgrowth located along the redwood's trunk, most often near the base of the tree. It's composed of dormant redwood stems. Saplings often sprout from a burl, and interestingly, the trees that grow out of the burl are clones; that is, they are genetically identical to the original tree. While the tree is alive and growing, a chemical "signal" keeps the burl dormant. If something stresses the tree—such as fire or insufficient rainfall—the burl will suddenly burst forth with new life. Experiments have shown that redwood burls kept in water will grow an array of branches. At the 1904 World's Fair in St. Louis, California's redwood display touted the beauty of burls, as noted by the May 19, 1904, *San Francisco Call*:

Burls are interesting: The redwood burl is the most prominent of the woods used in the [Fair's] exhibit. There are many Californians, even, who do not know just what this burl is. It is an immense knot that grows near the foot of many redwoods, some of them so large that boards several feet across can be cut from them. The redwood burl is very hard, beautifully colored and susceptible of a polish that dazzles the eye. No two are alike in the grain. The colorings are very warm and rich. Cut twenty thicknesses' to an inch, the polished burl makes a decorative veneer or panel that cannot be excelled. It is finding its way more and more into the interior decorations of homes belonging to wealthy people of taste, both in this country and in Europe, and the object of the display here is to still further familiarize the world with its beauties. . . . There is nothing more beautiful in all the Forestry building than this California display.

Burls are lumpy growths along the trunk of a redwood.
FRANK PATTERSON, PHOTOGRAPHER

Uniquely, the coastal redwood is also one of the fastest-growing trees in the world. The fact that a redwood can live to be two thousand years old—or older—makes it the titan of the tree world.

The greatest rate of growth for a redwood is gained during its first hundred years, perhaps thirty feet in the first twenty years; after that, it will average two to six feet in height plus an inch in diameter each year. After one or two hundred years, a redwood usually stands 200 to 350 feet high. After four hundred years, a redwood tree's trunk may average five to seven feet in diameter, but ten- to fifteen-foot trunks are possible.

After a thousand years, the redwood has thus gained most of its height in the first hundred years, and now grows mainly in width. At this point the mature redwood has lost many of its lower limbs, creating a broad canopy over the forest floor below. This canopy is one of the most important elements of a healthy redwood forest and provides shade, shelter, and protection for the diverse variety of plant, shrub, and animal life that lives beneath it. Although the shade may slow the growth of smaller redwoods, when conditions change with time, those trees will grow more quickly. At any rate, the shade is one of the characteristics of older groves. Visitors cannot help but notice the myriad ferns and blooming plants that thrive under the expanse of redwood canopy, plants that help hold moisture in the soil and create their own unique habitat.

As John Muir wrote so eloquently about the ferns: "There are wonderful ferneries about the misty waterfalls, some of the fronds ten feet high, others the most delicate of their tribe, the maidenhair fringing the rocks within reach of the lightest dust of the spray, while the shading trees on the cliffs above them, leaning over, look like eager listeners anxious to catch every tone of the restless waters."

In addition to its rate of growth and survivability, a redwood can grow a "new" set of roots if the soil level surrounding it rises, perhaps as a result of floods that inundate the area. Though the redwood forest soil is usually acidic and sandy, with a hardpan layer down a few feet, the redwood adapts to it, sending its roots out into the soil. One such redwood, estimated to be 1,200 years old, successfully sent out a new root system seven times, with a changing depth of soil totaling eleven feet. Likewise, because of the redwood's generally shallow root structure, a huge tree can easily topple during a major flood.

Coupled with its ability to establish new roots is the redwood's unique ability to compensate for a changing landscape caused by shifting slopes or earthquakes or collision with other trees. A redwood will "buttress" itself by sending out roots quickly on the underside or downhill side in order to stabilize itself and insure its survival.

Walking beneath the dizzying canopy created by the coastal redwoods' highest branches and leaves, it's hard to imagine that another world exists in the upper chambers of the forest. As recently as the 1990s, this rich diversity was relatively unknown and unexplored. Then researchers from California State University at Humboldt embarked on a study of the redwoods' complex crowns. What they found was stunning: All manner of flora and fauna live in the organic humus and pockets created by the branches growing vertically alongside the main trunk. Known as reiterated trunks, these ascending branches often act to stabilize the tree, all the while creating their own private environments.

It is definitely fitting that the California redwood was officially declared the state tree in April 1931. It is also fitting that the Redwood

The Redwood Highway, dedicated in 1923, opened the redwoods to the world.
FRANK PATTERSON, PHOTOGRAPHER

Highway, dedicated in 1923, became the first continuous automobile route from San Francisco to Crescent City and beyond. As noted by the *San Francisco Chronicle* in May 1928, "Nowhere else in the world can the sightseer find Redwood trees except in California. Nowhere else do these giant forests flourish!"

These silent, fog-shrouded forests have provided a haven for wildlife and plant species as well as a reservoir of resources for both the first humans—i.e., the diverse coastal Native American tribes who made the region their home for thousands of years—and the explorers, miners, loggers, and settlers who followed after.

As John Muir once wrote, "God has cared for these trees, saved them from drought, disease, avalanches, and a thousand tempests and floods," a reminder that the very presence of these thousand-year-old trees should humble us, making it imperative that we understand the rich cultural and physical link between man and redwood.

The Earth That Moves
Beneath the Trees

I was awakened by a tremendous earthquake, and though I had never before enjoyed a storm of this sort, the strange thrilling motion could not be mistaken, and I ran out of my cabin, both glad and frightened, shouting, 'A noble earthquake! A noble earthquake!'
—JOHN MUIR, *THE WILD MUIR: TWENTY-TWO OF JOHN MUIR'S GREATEST ADVENTURES*

"A ROAR AND THEN SUCCESSIVE SHOCKS EAST AND WEST TESTED THE workmanship of every structure in the county. Chimneys were shaken and the flying bricks damaged roofs and filled housewives with dismay. Furniture was dislodged. Even the heaviest pianos and bureaus found new spots to rest in. Dishes and bric-a-brac and many a dainty souvenir had to be gathered in a dustpan." So noted a reporter for the Humboldt County newspaper, *The Beacon*, on April 20, 1906, following the great earthquake that destroyed San Francisco and sent shocks all the way up the California coastline.

Meanwhile, the *Ferndale Enterprise* reported that the April 18, 1906, quake sent "a shock [or earthquake], unparalleled for severity in the history of this county, [hitting] Humboldt [last] Wednesday morning at about 5:15 o'clock. The tremblor, in the few seconds during which its force was felt, caused damage which will run up into the thousands of dollars in Ferndale alone, to say nothing of the other points visited by it."

Another reporter noted, "The fine new brick store of the Russ, Early and Williams Co., completed but a few months ago probably presents the sorriest spectacle. The front of this building was completely demolished, the bricks being thrown into the street, while the thick plate glass was reduced to fragments. The walls were also cracked and broken."

The earthquake registered 7.7 and 7.9 and stretched for more than 290 miles, and it lasted between forty-five and sixty seconds. It was an event that became a landmark in California's history, and those who experienced it were deeply shaken.

Chinese Joss House, San Francisco, Cal.

Chinatown before the 1906 earthquake that destroyed much of the city.
FRITZ-MULLER

Likewise, those who have experienced any of California's more recent earthquakes remain deeply aware of the movement that lies just below the surface of the ground upon which we walk. But most of us give it little thought, and as the nearly 1.25 million annual tourists meander the trails and pathways of the Redwood National and State Parks' forests, the mystic tranquility of the region belies its more dangerous character; that is, that the northern California coastline is the most seismically active area in the state.

So what makes the area so vulnerable to shocks and tremors?

Three major faults come together in an area identified as the Mendocino Triple Junction; they act as the boundaries of three distinct tectonic plates. These tectonic plates (thin pieces of the earth's crust) are known as the North American, the Pacific, and the Gorda and lie offshore near Cape Mendocino, only a hundred miles southwest of Redwood National Park.

The plates slide against each other along the fault lines that border them as they move in opposite directions. Indeed, this entire coastal region was created when the Pacific and Gorda plates collided, pushing the sediments from the "disintegrating" plates upward to create a new land mass.

Occasionally this movement still erupts in the form of earthquakes—some small, some large. During the 1906 earthquake, land on the west side of the rift jumped as much as twenty feet to the north/northwest.

The Pacific Plate relative to the North American Plate is moving north, and the "boundary" between them is the San Andreas Fault. Californians are familiar with the San Andreas Fault, which is 650 to 700 miles long with depths of about 10 miles. It is a transform fault, meaning that as pressure builds as the Pacific Plate moves, the massive release of energy is felt as earthquakes by those of us standing onshore.

A second plate boundary is the Mendocino Fault, which runs west from the mouth of the Mattole River and perpendicular to the San Andreas Fault. The Pacific Plate and the Gorda Plate collide along this fault line; that is, as the larger Pacific Plate moves northward, the Gorda Plate moves eastward. The two plates collide, generating hundreds of earthquakes every year.

The most important fault in this region is the Cascadia Subduction Zone, which runs about seven hundred miles north from the Triple Junction. A subduction event along this fault is particularly capable of generating a tsunami, and estimates suggest that such an event could create a trans-Pacific tsunami with waves between thirty and ninety feet. Geologic records indicate that tsunamis of this sort likely occurred in the area in 1900 BC, 1100 BC, 900 BC, AD 400, AD 700, and AD 900.

In Humboldt County, many of the earthquakes are caused by the Juan de Fuca Plate system that lies under the North American Plate about a hundred miles out in the Pacific Ocean. Because of its location, there is generally less damage done in areas such as Humboldt versus areas surrounding the San Francisco Bay or other points south.

However, according to researchers at Humboldt State University and the University of Southern California, Crescent City (in Del Norte County, twenty miles south of the Oregon border) has experienced tsunami conditions thirty-one times in the years 1933 to 2008. Although many of these tsunamis were barely perceptible by people, eleven times the wave measurements actually exceeded one meter, while four times there was some damage. At least one of the tsunamis to hit the northern coastline was considered a major event.

When measuring earthquakes, scientists consider two types of vibrations: compression waves and transverse or shear waves. Compression waves, also called P-waves, travel faster. The transverse or shear waves, also called S-waves, travel more slowly. People recognize the P-wave as a sharp thud, or shock. The S-wave arrives next and feels more like a rolling or swaying sensation.

But the region is not only a seismic area. The region surrounding the Redwood National Forest is also part of the Cascade Volcanic Arc that extends from northern California to the coastal mountains of British Columbia. Fossilized redwood, dating back three million years, was found near Santa Rosa, fifty miles north of California's Muir Woods, a testimony to the long history of the area's potential volcanic activity. This area is home to several stratovolcanoes, including these major peaks:

In California: Lassen Peak, which last erupted from 1914 to 1917; Mount Shasta; and Medicine Lake, located near Tule Lake

In Oregon: Three Sisters; Mount Jefferson (also known as Mount Pitt); Crater Lake, which was created when Mount Mazama collapsed thousands of years ago; and Mount Hood

In Washington: Mount Adams; Mount St. Helens, which last erupted in 1980; Mount Rainier; Glacier Peak; and Mount Baker

In British Columbia, Canada: Mount Garibaldi and Mount Meagher

In addition to earthquakes, the region surrounding Redwood National Park has been hit by tsunamis. One famous tsunami hit Crescent City on March 28, 1964—the aftermath of the great Alaskan earthquake of 1964. The wave did great damage to the city, where twenty-nine blocks were laid to ruin. Damage ran up to $17 million.

It's now known that earthquakes that occur offshore within the Cascadia Subduction Zone can cause tsunamis. Based on carbon dating of local tsunami deposits, a major earthquake occurred in 1700, with an estimated magnitude of 8.7 to 9.2. The offshore Pacific quake caused thirty-foot-high waves to rush inland, causing damage not only along the California-Oregon-Washington coastline, but also across the Pacific to Japan. Japanese records verify that a tsunami did indeed strike Japan on January 26, 1700.

In 2008 seismologists noted more than six hundred quakes over a ten-day period approximately 150 miles southwest of Newport, Oregon. The quakes did not follow the normal pattern of a large quake, followed by aftershocks. The scientists described the sounds heard through hydrophones as being similar to peals of thunder.

Although the scientific community has only recently identified the seismic activity of the Cascadia Subduction Zone, Native American oral traditions make it clear that the region's tribes were familiar with earthquakes. In the *Bulletin of the Seismological Society of America* (1985), T. H. Heaton and P. D. Snavely suggested a number of tsunamis have hit the Pacific coastline and have been recorded in various Native American legends. The tsunami of 1700 no doubt destroyed many tribal villages located up and down the California coast, according to Ruth S. Ludwin of the University of Washington, Pacific Northwest Seismograph Network.

As a way of recording major historical events, as well as a way of understanding the events, tsunamis, earthquakes, and other disasters are often woven into the oral traditions and stories of many tribes. The Yurok, along with several coastal northwestern tribes, have passed down a popular myth, that of the battle between Thunderbird (the wind) and Whale (water). T. T. Waterman recorded an account of an early earthquake told by a Yurok woman, Annie of Espeu. She reported:

> *Then he [Earthquake] started and arrived there at Pulekuk, he and his companion.... He thought, "I will try ... Look at this. Here it is easy"—speaking to his companion—"It will be easy to do that, to sink this prairie. So I shall do that first," said Earthquake. And he said, "Very well." So he ran around a little and the ground sank, there at Pulekuk ... and then from there they went south. They said, "We shall have to go there: we two shall go together." They went south first and sank the ground. They were still together, those that [later] went back into the mountains. So they went south with one another. And then he did that: he repeatedly caused the ground to sink to the south. He kept sinking it: every little while there would be another earthquake, and then another earthquake: that is what he was doing. And then the water filled those places, the water coming from the mountains, at Osig.*

How Native Americans' Roots Are Connected to the Redwoods

When the blood in your veins returns to the sea,
and the earth in your bones returns to the ground,
perhaps then you will remember that this land does not belong to you,
it is you who belong to this land.

—NATIVE AMERICAN QUOTE

PEOPLE HAVE BEEN PART OF REDWOOD NATIONAL PARK'S UNWRITTEN history for generations. Although estimates vary, there is clear archaeological evidence suggesting that people were living in the region of the redwood forests for thousands of years, perhaps when many of today's mammoth sentinels were yet seedlings. As a result, their histories are deeply linked to the redwoods.

It's estimated that at least fifteen different tribal groups originally inhabited the northern California coastline. Although they belonged to different linguistic groups, their cultures were similar in the way they responded to living in and depending upon the Tall Trees. Most lived in villages and relied on the rivers, prairies, and meadows, cultivating the redwood forests for food, building materials, and boats.

Modern-day tribes, principally the Tolowa, Yurok, and Chilula, are among the principal groups with strong ties to the parks' region, although a number of other coastal tribes used redwood in their material culture, including the Wiyot, Hupa, and Karuk. The Pomo and Sinkyone also built small houses of bark, and Pomo women designed skirts made of shredded bark from redwood, while they and other tribes wove baskets using redwood root fibers or redwood bark.

The three tribes most closely linked to the Redwood National and State Parks, however, include: the Yurok, who settled in the central area near the Klamath River; the Tolowa, who settled along the Smith River; and the Chilula, who settled principally along Redwood Creek. Geographically, their early villages were often isolated by the natural impediments such as rivers, canyons, cliffs, and forests, but the coastal tribes often traded back and forth with the inland tribes. The redwoods thus provided both protection and resource for them, and they lived intimately with the Tall Trees.

According to Alfred L. Kroeber, the larger villages were usually located near prime foraging locations, including estuaries and river mouths, or along protected coastal areas. Smaller villages were often established when larger villages became too populated.

In 1852 a census revealed that the Yurok tribe was the most numerous of the region's indigenous peoples. Of Algonkin language heritage, the Yurok built villages along the Klamath River and the Trinity (the Klamath's largest tributary) and near lagoons along the Pacific Ocean coastline. The Yurok—which comes from the Karuk word *yuruk* and was a name given to them—originally called themselves simply Olekwo'l ("persons") or *Oohl*, meaning "Indian people." Yurok downriver on the Klamath were referred to as *Pue-lik-lo'* ("downriver Indian"), while those on the Trinity River and upper Klamath River were called *Pey-cheek-lo'* ("upriver Indian") and those on the coast were called *Ner-'er-ner'* ("coast Indian").

According to Axel R. Lindgren in the introduction to T. T. Waterman's *Yurok Geography*, first published in 1920 by the University of California Press, Berkeley, and republished in 1993: "The geographical location of the prehistoric homeland of the Yurok was a narrow strip of land which paralleled the Pacific Rim along the shores of Northwestern California for ninety miles. The southern boundary was Little River; the northern boundary, the Wilson Creek Basin."

There were no less than fifty Yurok villages at one time throughout the region. The people were considered some of the greatest fishermen and canoe makers.

As noted by Waterman in *Yurok Geography*, the Yurok "occupied the lower thirty-six miles of the Klamath River, from a short distance above the point where the Trinity enters it, to the sea, and a somewhat longer stretch of seacoast, reaching northward to Wilson Creek, Del Norte County, and southward to Trinidad Bay, in Humboldt County, a distance of forty-two miles."

The Yurok, as well as the Wiyot, Karuk, Chilula, and Tolowa, built rectangular or square redwood split-plank houses with pitched roofs and chimneys. These buildings often measured eighteen to twenty-five feet square, or twenty feet long. The planks, usually split from fallen or driftwood logs (called *keehl* by the Yurok), were several inches thick and perhaps one to four feet wide; they were set on edge vertically to form walls, while the floor was excavated to about three feet below ground level. Two rows of planks were used in building the walls, one row inside the other; the roof was also a double layer of boards or planks set against the walls and on top of ridgepoles.

A central fire pit was positioned in the center or near-center of the house, and a large opening in the roof served as a smoke hole. A front entrance was also a hole, either round or square, and often located off-center. Those with greater wealth often laid plank- or clay-covered floors; otherwise, the homes had dirt floors.

The Yurok also built sweathouses and larger "assembly halls" out of redwood planks or rough boards cut from fallen trees. Sweathouses were smaller than family houses, perhaps twelve feet long, and fully subterranean. Occasionally the pitched roof was covered in earth; generally there were three family houses grouped around a single sweathouse. The sweathouse was the principal residence of men and post-pubescent boys, and women were rarely allowed access unless there was a special ceremony.

Within the boundaries of today's Redwood National and State Parks, anthropologists have estimated that at least 2,500 Yurok residents lived in established villages, including the villages of Rekwoi, Wetkwau, Tsekwetl, Pegwolau, Keskitsa, Tmeri, and Otwego. Other sites identified near or in the park's boundaries include important ceremonial locations. At each of these locations there was a sacred redwood sweathouse.

Today the Yurok number five thousand, making them the largest tribe in California.

Historically the Tolowa (*Taa-laa-wa Dee-ni'*) were located along the Smith River and today's Jedediah Smith Redwoods State Park, whose "occupational history" most likely spans 8,500 years. Those who lived traditionally on the Smith River were known as *Gee Dee-ni'* (upriver Tolowa), while those who lived downriver at the mouth of the Smith River were known as *Da'-chvn-dvn Dee-ni'*.

Most of the Tolowa settlements were located along the coast and estuary, and included such villages identified as Troolet, Howonquet, Tatatun, Tatitun, MesLteLtun, Etchulet, TucRockuctun, and Ltrucme. In addition, their place of origin was considered to be Yontocket, a village site located near the mouth of the Smith River where the people came together for World Renewal (*Ne-Dosh*) dances and other ceremonies.

The Smith River is a shorter watershed, approximately thirty-two "air miles" inland from the coast. According to Shannon Tushingham, research associate from the University of California, Davis, who worked with the California Department of Parks and Recreation Archaeology, History and Museums Division, the headwaters of the river is located in the nearby Siskiyou mountains, "flowing first through the Oak Woodland mixed hardwood zone and Klamath mountains, then west through an approximately ten-mile-wide redwood belt, and finally through a four-mile-wide flat coastal strip where it meanders for approximately eight miles before emptying into the Pacific Ocean."

The Tolowa inhabited Tolowa villages along the coast for much of the year, particularly during the rainy season. In late summer, families would travel and make temporary camps along the coast as they fished for smelt; the families who camped there each year, however, owned these sites. Late summer was also the time of year when men would gather and form groups to hunt offshore. Finally, from September to mid or late November, families would travel inland to fish for salmon and gather acorns.

As with other coastal tribes, Tolowa villages were autonomous, and there was no "Tolowa tribe" per se. In fact, *Tolowa* is actually a Yurok and Hupa word, which was (according to Kroeber) adopted from the name of a village originally located at Lake Earl named Tolokwe.

In a number of ways the Tolowa resemble the Hupa and the Yurok and were greatly influenced by the sea. In excavations at Tolowa sites, archaeologists have uncovered the earliest redwood plank houses, the earliest evidence of tobacco smoking in the Pacific Northwest coast region, and the only semi-subterranean sweathouse recorded in northwestern California. Further cooperative research is ongoing under a partnership established between the Tolowa, UC Davis, and Redwood National and State Parks. It encompasses the area identified as the Jedediah Smith Campground and Hiouchi Flat, although much of what is now Del Norte County lies within the ancestral territories of the Tolowa.

Meanwhile the Wiyot were originally located from Mad River through Humboldt Bay to the lower Eel River. Their language, like the Yurok, is related to the Algonquian linguistic group.

The Chilula—or Redwood Creek Indians—are an Athabascan tribe. Generally located along the coastline, in the summer and fall they moved to the prairies of the Bald Hills. *Chilula* is the English version of *Tsulu-la*, or the "people of Tsulu (the Bald Hills)," but there has been much debate over their correct name. Minni Reeves, in an interview in 1976, related

The Wiyot settled along the coast, from Mad River to the lower Eel River.
CHARLES PAYNE, FRANK PAYNE (ART-RAY), PHOTOGRAPHERS

that their tribal name was actually *Kixunai-ho-e-ch-ket*, which means "people from within the redwood tree." The early villages of the Chilula were located along Redwood Creek from near Orick, on the northwest, to the area known as Stover Ranch, on the southeast; in fact, all but one of their villages were located on the east side of Redwood Creek, where it was slightly less densely forested. Two of their eighteen historic villages were located within Redwood National Park's boundaries.

The climate within the Redwood Creek basin is characterized by fog throughout the year. Although it occasionally snows on the adjacent ranges, including the Bald Hills, very little if any snow falls along the creek, but precipitation, in the form of rain—and even torrential rain—occurs in the fall, winter, and spring.

Much of the area here features prairie and oak woodlands; it's been suggested that the Chilula burned these areas purposely to preserve the open space. This helped to insure that the people could maintain an environment that supported game, such as elk and deer, as well as the plants that they collected, including acorns and hazelnuts. At one time the Chilula population was calculated to have totaled at least six hundred individuals.

Like the Yurok and Wiyot, the Chilula also built redwood plank houses and small square sweathouses. The Chilula were the most southerly coastal Athabascan tribe to use this kind of sweathouse. When they moved up into the hills during the drier months, they built square huts of redwood bark slabs.

Native American Mythology and Redwoods

Not only is redwood an element of tribal material culture, but the tall trees are clearly linked to tribal spiritual life as well. Indeed, according to Edwin C. Bearss in *Redwood National Park: History/Basic Data*, "A house was understood to be a living being. The redwood that formed its planks was itself the body of one of the Spirit Beings. Spirit Beings were believed to be a divine race who existed before humans in the redwood region and who taught people the proper way to live here."

In one legend, during a season of drought, one tribe was forced to move upriver, to the mouth of the Mad River—which was home to another tribe. The two tribes began warring until the Great Spirit demanded the leaders sit below a specific redwood tree, after which he promised rain would fall on the first tribe's homeland. When the two bands conducted a peace treaty, the tree became a place of great significance. To mark the site, whenever men of either tribe passed the tree, they would shoot an arrow into its trunk, and women would push small green branches into the furrows of its redwood bark. Supposedly, in the 1880s, a fire consumed most of the tree, but "Indian Arrow Tree" still stands—a burned snag—in memory of this important event.

The Chilula believe that large, burned-out hollow redwoods are sacred places, and that the Creator moved in and out of the physical and spirit world through these hollowed trees. The "Dancing Doctor Rock," however, was probably the most important religious site in Chilula territory.

According to Earle Goddard Pliny in his *Notes on the Chilula Indians of Northwestern California* the Dancing Doctor Rock is "a rocky point on the top of the ridge about a mile northeast of Lyon's house . . . used as a dancing place for those who were training to become shamans." Here, according to Kroeber's notes, practicing shamans were "required to fast, seek a vision, lament for power, then sing and dance upon this rock in order to acquire the 'doctor pain' necessary for healing power."

The Yurok also consider the redwood tree a sacred and living creature. Kroeber recorded one Yurok myth, about the origin of boats. A summary of it follows:

> *Sky-Owner, or Pulekukwerek, asked, "What shall we do that persons may cross [the river]?"*
>
> *Suddenly, someone spoke up. "That is what I came for. I can be used for boats. They will make boats of me and cross the river."*
>
> *Then Pulekukwerek asked, "What is your name?"*
>
> *The newcomer replied, "I am called Redwood."*
>
> *Pulekukwerek said, "It is good that you grew so quickly. Now persons will live [properly]."*

Redwood said, "I want them to put pitch on my head. I want them to put pitch on my stern. I want a withe [used to tie the boat, also called a 'necklace'] around my neck. That is the way I like it."

Another Yurok legend recorded by Kroeber spoke of a flood where "the ocean covered the earth. That is why there are redwood logs on the high ridges. . . . Two men and two women were saved in a boat; all others drowned. Sky-Owner gave them a song. When they sang, the water receded."

The historic center of the world for the Yurok is located at the village site of Kepel, located between two "subdivisions" of upriver and downriver villages on the Klamath River, "a few miles below the point where the Trinity comes in from the south." This place, according to Waterman, the Yurok call *qe'nek*.

It was here that the sky was made:

A character called we'sona-me'gtol *("world-maker"), fashioned the empyrean vault after the manner and pattern of a fish-net. He took a rope and laid it down in an enormous circle, leaving one end loose at a certain place among the hills. Traveling off in a gigantic circuit and coming around from the south to the same spot again, he joined the two ends of the rope together. Then for days he journeyed back and forth over the hills, filling in and knotting the strands across each other. The song he sang to accompany his labors is still sung by people who work on fishnets or netted carrying-bags. When the sky-net was complete, the hero took hold of it in two places and threw it up. As it sailed aloft it became solid, and now stretches over us as the great blue sky. Above this solid sky there is a sky-country, wo'noiyik, about the topography of which the Yurok's ideas are almost as definite as are his ideas of southern Mendocino County, for instance. Down-stream from qe'nek, at a place called qe'nek-pul, qe'neck, is an invisible ladder leading up to the sky-country. A great number of "myth people" who formerly congregated at qe'nek, quite frequently went up this ladder to watch shinny games in the sky-country.*

Axel Lindgren, of Yurok descent, also introduces the reader to the Yurok's close connection to the land and its relationship to the Yurok's spiritual world when he writes:

A number of promontories and sea stacks have inundated caves, which are homes of Spirits who control the tides, sea storms, and the entrance of rivers into the ocean. When Spirits sleep in a fetal position, the river will parallel the breaker-line for two or three miles before emptying into the ocean as Mad and Little River do now. In the northern part of the Yurok territory the mighty Klamath shows the same pattern. If Spirits sleep with legs extended, the rivers will flow directly into the sea as all three rivers did for many years.

For the Karuk, also spelled Kiruk and Karok ("upriver" people), the center of their world is located on the Klamath at the mouth of the Salmon River, at the site of their sacred village known as *Ishipishi*. For them the world was created by *Ik-hareya*, who sent the salmon upriver each spring.

THE TRIBES AND THEIR LINKS TO THE REDWOODS

The early coastal tribes all used redwood. They built redwood stools, storage boxes, and even sweathouse "pillows," as well as various fishing tools and traps. Other construction technologies incorporating redwood in their designs included "check" dams built and installed to slow or stop the flow of water in order to trap fish; carved effigies of one's enemies; graves lined with redwood planks; and using redwood bark and/or root fibers in basket-making or in the decoration of women's skirts and men's ceremonial mantles.

Most famous are the redwood canoes built by the tribes, particularly the Yurok, Tolowa, and Wiyot. Because life was centered at the mouths of rivers or up and down the wild rivers, canoes were vital to the tribe's survival, and there is still a great deal of spirituality connected to them. In fact, redwood trees are considered living beings and thought to stand as "guardians" over sacred places. Canoes are spoken to or sung to, especially in dangerous or difficult circumstances. Songs and formulas are said to

Standing on the rocks, a Hupa fisherman watches for salmon.

keep the water smooth. The canoe is also important in the White Deer-skin Dance, an important traditional ceremony.

Canoes were originally made from downed or drift redwood logs recovered from the rivers. Although there is some evidence to suggest smaller redwood trees were occasionally cut down, that was the exception. A selected log was burned into canoe length and then split with adzes or other tools. To hollow out the log, pitch was spread over the area and set on fire; to control the amount of fire, the flames were smothered with green bark. The finished canoe was polished using stones. Tools were made of stone, shell—such as mussel shells—or elk horn.

The Yurok used canoes to travel up and down the Klamath River and the coast of California for trading, fishing, and hunting. Carving a canoe was a difficult, tedious job, often taking months, but the final product lasted for years and was an integral part of the material culture of all the coastal tribes. Canoe makers (called *yoch* by the Yurok) were revered as great craftsmen.

Canoes were also occasionally traded with inland tribes—e.g., the Hupa—and brought a high price. Even the first white settlers to the area were known to purchase canoes from the tribes. Most dugout canoes measured about eighteen feet long, were squared off at the ends, and were designed to navigate the swifter running water of the area's salmon-filled rivers. Longer canoes, often measuring thirty feet or more, were paddled out to sea for deep-water fishing and seal hunting.

One Yurok-style redwood canoe is on display at the Orick-area Red-wood National Park visitor center. It was carved by Yurok elders Dewey George and Jimmy James, with the help of Jimmy James Jr. and Chuck Donahue. The canoe was originally commissioned in 1968 by Mr. and Mrs. Chester Paul to display at Paul's Cannery in Klamath, California. In 1987 it was donated to the park by Mrs. Paul.

According to T. T. Waterman:

They [the Yurok] paddled all along the cliffs near the harbors, and around all the nearer sea rocks, to gather mussels and to hunt sea lions. In calm weather they frequently voyaged out to Redding rock, which lies six miles offshore. This really was a bold feat, for the rock offered

A Hupa fisherman paddles a redwood canoe downriver.
PHOTOGRAPH BY EDWARD S. CURTIS, LIBRARY OF CONGRESS

no shelter, and if a squall came up they had to paddle for shore at the risk of being swamped. Sometimes, when weather was favorable, the Yurok canoeman boldly made the voyage from port to port on the open sea.

More often than not, however, tribes fished at the mouth of a river, where men would stand at the edge of the surf with nets, spears, or wooden fish traps.

Paddles, also carved from redwood, were stout poles about six to eight feet long with narrow, heavy blades at the end. Men stood up and navigated using the long poles; only one man, the helmsman, sat at the head of the canoe with a traditional paddle.

In addition, according to U.S.F.S. records, "Scattered accounts of Indians who lived in redwood cavities may reflect a common if only seasonal custom. Early in the 20th century one of the few surviving Lolangkok Sinkyone stated that he was born in a redwood hollow in Humboldt Redwoods State Park, where his family spent the winter. Other families lived in fire cavities in Redwood National Park as recently as the late 19th century" (redwood.forestthreats.org/native.htm).

COMPARATIVE CULTURAL TRADITIONS OF THE REGION'S TRIBES

The clothing worn by the Klamath region's tribes was often similar. Women wore skirts made from the inner bark of the maple or from redwood fibers and/or roots. Bark was stripped and then beaten until the inner bark separated from the rough outer bark. In addition, the skirts were decorated with strips or strings of pine nuts, seeds, shells, and occasionally beads obtained through trade.

Women sometimes also wore skirts of buckskin cut into strips, decorated again with pine nuts. The nuts and seeds or shells made a pleasing sound when they walked. Around the body women also wore a belt made of animal hair, shells, porcupine quills, and dentalia. Most tribal women also wore caps woven from grass, fern, quills, and other natural materials.

The Chilula were principally a hunting and gathering people in contrast to the Hupa or Yurok. According to Goddard, "The heavy redwood forests to the west were frequented by herds of elk and the half timbered ridges to the east were especially favorable to deer." Elk hunts were often organized by gathering together either family members or others of the tribe; and, while acorn patches were considered personal property, hunting grounds were communal property.

Only the men hunted, but boys were included as part of their training, and before any hunt, the men entered the sweathouse (constructed of redwood planks) to "purify" themselves.

Because salmon was a primary food source, fishing tools were sophisticated and varied. Kroeber, in his research, noted that harpoons were used along river outlets or bars; weirs, spears, dip nets, and gaffs were used in shallow water; harpoons, gaffs, and traps were used in riffles; nets set on platforms were used in eddies; "plunge" nets, traps, harpoons, gaffs, and baskets were used at falls or in cascading water; bow and arrow, snares, poison, and "sturgeon riding" or diving were techniques used in deep pools of water; and short weirs with basket traps, hook and line, and "sniggling" were used in creeks and small streams.

The Chilula who fished at Noledin Falls or up and down Redwood Creek used harpoons occasionally. They were made of deer and elk antler. Chilula dip nets were made from hazelwood and fir, which was hardened in fire, and the loop net bags were made from iris grass fibers, gathered by women but prepared by the men.

The Chilula also trapped eels in weirs. According to Kroeber, "At some point on a small stream, perhaps twenty feet wide, where the water was three to five feet deep, heavy posts were driven vertically into the stream bed at about six feet intervals... Next a matting, woven of split sections of poles, was rolled out on the upriver side of this framework, and finally leafy boughs weighted with stone were placed along the bottom of the weir."

Pottery was not a characteristic of the coastal tribes, but basket-making was. Baskets were used for storage, eating, cooking, grinding,

Hupa fisherman checking a weir on the Trinity River.
PHOTOGRAPH BY EDWARD S. CURTIS, LIBRARY OF CONGRESS

A Karuk woman stirs something in a mush basket.

gathering, and carrying things, and were even used as women's caps. Some baskets were so tightly woven they could hold water. Gathering materials required patience, and they had to be prepared before they could be used. Living near or in the redwood forests made these materials easy to find.

As to the relationship between coastal tribes and the redwoods, it may have been best described by Minni Reeves, Chilula tribal elder and religious leader, Hupa Indian Reservation:

> *The redwood trees are sacred. They are a special gift and reminder from the Great Creator to the human beings. The Great Creator made everything, including trees of all kinds, but he wanted to leave a special gift for his children. So he took a little medicine from each tree, he said a prayer and sang a powerful song, and then he mixed it with the blood of our people. He left it on Earth as a demonstration of his love for his children. The redwood trees have a lot of power: they are the tallest, live the longest, and are the most beautiful trees in the world. Destroy these trees and you destroy the Creator's love. And if you destroy that which the Creator loves so much, you will eventually destroy mankind.*

First Contact: How Life in the Forest Began to Change

We need the tonic of wildness. . . . At the same time that we are earnest to explore and learn all things, we require that all things be mysterious and unexplorable, that land and sea be indefinitely wild, unsurveyed and unfathomed by us because it is unfathomable. We can never have enough of nature.

—HENRY DAVID THOREAU,
WALDEN; OR, LIFE IN THE WOODS

THE FIRST "FOREIGN" CONTACT WITH THE NORTHERN COAST OF CALIfornia came with the Spanish explorers. Juan Rodríguez Cabrillo is believed to have been the first European to explore the Pacific coastline of California. Though possibly of Portuguese descent, Cabrillo sailed for the Spanish and led an expedition in June 1542 up from Mexico to San Diego Bay. He continued north and it is generally believed he sailed as far north as Point Reyes, north of San Francisco. Unfortunately, Cabrillo then died, leaving his crew to carry on. Many historians believe the crew sailed as far north as the Rogue River on the Oregon coast.

One tantalizing tale, which has yet to be documented, involves a Chinese sailor, Hee-li, who may have navigated the Pacific to Monterey—two thousand years *before* the Spanish. According to his writings, he inadvertently sailed east when he thought he was sailing west. The error was made, as the story goes, when a cockroach got lodged under the needle of his compass, but the mistake was not discovered until one of Hee-li's men cleaned the compass sometime later. Meanwhile, their small vessel touched shore, and Hee-li and his men explored this new land for several weeks. This is when they saw and marveled at huge "red" trees.

When Hee-li finally returned home, he wrote of his adventures, which was kept in an archive at Si-Ngan-Foo. The document was then "discovered" by an American missionary who searched for the account in 1890 and translated it. Whether the account is true or not will never be known, but therein lies the fascinating notion that much of what has not been documented may actually be true!

There is a suggestion that the first European to see the redwood forests was Fray Juan Crespi in 1769, and the first to enter the area of Redwood National Park were Spanish explorers Don Bruno de Heceta and Juan Francisco de la Bodega y Cuadra in 1775. Under the flag of Spain, their exploring party sailed up the Pacific coastline, but they did not establish any population centers, although it's been reported that Heceta and Cuadra did encounter the people of the Yurok village of Chue-rey, laying claim to the area at Trinidad Head by erecting a cross.

It was after Russian fur traders began moving down from Alaska in 1765 that the Spanish Crown began encouraging settlement through the offer of land grants, called ranchos, where cattle and sheep were raised.

Likewise, the British sailed the coastline, but the lack of natural ports kept these early expeditions from moving inland. One of the most famous British explorers of the eighteenth century, Captain James Cook, circumnavigated the globe twice before setting his course for the North Pacific Ocean. Although he's most often recognized for his explorations of the South Pacific and the Hawaiian Islands (where he was killed), Cook also braved the frozen Arctic searching for a northern route to Asia. On his journey, he sailed along the Pacific coast aboard his ship, the HMS *Resolution*, in 1778 and successfully mapped the coastline all the way from California up to the Bering Strait.

It was British explorer George Vancouver who, from 1791 to 1795, explored and charted North America's northwestern Pacific coast regions, including the coasts of Alaska, British Columbia, Washington, and Oregon. He, too, explored the Hawaiian Islands as well as the southwest coast of Australia. In Canada, both Vancouver Island and the city of Vancouver are named in his honor, as is Vancouver, Washington. During his expeditions he was ordered to survey every inlet and outlet on the west coast of the mainland, all the way north to Alaska. Most of this detailed work was done while propelling a small boat, either by sail or oar.

In response to the budding interest displayed by the British and Russians, Spain began to expand its control over California by establishing a powerful chain of Catholic missions. By 1823 there were twenty-one.

The Adams-Onis Treaty of 1819 set Spain's northern boundary at the 42nd parallel, which would one day become the established boundary between Oregon and California.

THE RUSSIANS AND FORT ROSS

While Great Britain was settling the Atlantic coastline, Russian explorers, trappers, and settlers traveled east into Siberia. In 1639 they reached the Pacific Ocean. By the mid-seventeenth century, frontier Russians had discovered a route from the Arctic Ocean into the Pacific. In 1741 they discovered the Aleutian Islands and Alaska and claimed them for Russia. By 1760 both Spain and Britain were growing concerned about Russia's toehold on the Pacific Northwest. Spain began sending expeditions to the north and established its hold on California through its chain of missions, while Britain sent Captain Cook on an expedition to discover the Northwest Passage. However, in spite of the profits being made by Russian fur-trading companies, the number of such companies began to decline, in part because of the declining animal numbers as well as the costs involved in traveling from the Siberian coast to the Pacific Rim. In 1781 the strongest Russian companies reorganized to become the Russian-American Company.

The company was given a number of tasks, including exploring and colonizing unoccupied territory plus exploiting mineral resources in those areas. The Russian-American Company literally controlled all Russian trade, exploration, and settlement in North America. The unfortunate decline in otter numbers in Alaskan waters compelled the company to send a hunting expedition down to California in 1803; partnering with an American, Joseph O'Cain, the party sailed south as far as Baja California. There they found otter aplenty. Unfortunately the Russian settlement did not fare well, and the inability to raise crops or stock left the people nearly starving. The winter of 1805–06 was so severe that no supply ships were able to bring any relief. The people suffered and many died.

Nikolai Petrovich Rezanov, the Russian imperial chamberlain, was sent to inspect the settlement. The situation was so distressing that Rezanov bought a ship from Americans in Alaska and sailed to San Francisco in hopes of obtaining grain. Although trade with foreigners was forbidden, the enterprising Rezanov managed not only to anchor, but also to meet with Presidio Commandant José Argüello.

Rezanov returned to Sitka with provisions for the people and then set sail for St. Petersburg. On his departure he left instructions with Baranov to cultivate "the one unoccupied stretch" of the northern California coastline. He hoped Baranov could establish enough of a settlement that food and provisions would refill Sitka's coffers. Unfortunately Rezanov contracted a fever, and after falling from his horse, died on March 1, 1807.

Meanwhile, Baranov sent Ivan Kuskov, his deputy, on a series of expeditions south to "New Albion," the name first given California by Sir Francis Drake. Kuskov established a temporary headquarters at Bodega Bay, or "Rumiantsev Bay," north of San Francisco. In 1811 he selected a site rich in soil, timber (including driftwood logs and fallen trees), water, and pasture. He paid the local tribe three blankets, two axes, three hoes, and some beads and clothing for the land. Twenty-five Russians and eighty Native Alaskans arrived to build the outpost.

The remote, all-redwood "fort" was completed in August 1812. The stockade was built of redwood timbers, with surrounding walls that measured 250 by 300 feet in length. The timbers used to construct the walls stood 15 feet high. Two blockhouses with cannon ports were built at the northwest and southeast corners. Cannon were positioned around the fort and sentries stationed at each blockhouse. However, the settlement was principally a commercial center, not a military one. The fort was given the name "Ross"—a derivation of Russia ("Rossiia"). It was called Ross Colony, Ross Settlement, Ross Fortress, and Ross Office, but the Americans referred to it as "Fort Ross."

Outside the walls of the fort were constructed a windmill, cattle yard, bakery, threshing floor, and cemetery, farm buildings and bathhouses, an orchard, and a vegetable garden. Along the inlet were a shipyard, forge, tannery, boathouse, and storage sheds.

Although no formal accounts of daily life at the fort exist, accounts left by residents and visitors point to a simple but busy lifestyle. Fishing, hunting, farming, and ranching consumed most of the colonists' time. Not once was the settlement threatened by outside attack.

The Russian settlement was extremely fortunate in that the surrounding forests provided redwood, fir, and oak—raw materials for housing, shipbuilding, and other products. The colonists made barrels out of redwood and sawed redwood beams, some twenty-plus feet long, for construction purposes and also for sale to the Californios. This is likely some of the first marketing achieved with regard to the coastal redwood.

With so much timber available, company officials pursued shipbuilding, and in 1817 employed a shipwright from Sitka to come and supervise the construction. The fort's craftsmen did manage to build three brigs and a schooner, ranging in size from 160 to 200 tons, but not long after that, shipbuilding was abandoned because the oak used in construction was, according to "Historic California Posts, Camps, Stations and Airfields: Fort Ross (Fort Rossiya)," "freshly cut and . . . unseasoned, and by the time the ship was launched the rot had set in. After three or four years the changes in climate caused the rot to increase in all the main parts of the ship, and there was no way to repair it."

In the end, the larger vessels were used primarily for coastal sea trade. However, Fort Ross's shipbuilding enterprise was the first of any size to operate in California.

After Mexico won its independence from Spain in 1821 and trade with foreigners was no longer outlawed, Russian trade suffered, and by 1839 the officials of the Russian-American Company decided to abandon the colony at Ross.

In the end, John Sutter agreed to buy the fort and all its buildings, livestock, and implements—but not the land, which was under Mexican control. Thus, on January 1, 1842, about one hundred colonists, including Native Alaskans, sailed out of Bodega Bay. After thirty years, the emblematic Russian-American Company's flag was lowered and Russia's control over "the one unoccupied stretch" of California coastline was abandoned.

JEDEDIAH SMITH

Though travel and exploration occurred along California's rugged northern coast in the early 1800s, there was little interaction with the tribes living there except for some trade. The Spanish, British, Russian, and American trappers were far more interested in seal pelts or beaver pelts than redwoods. They frequently exchanged trade goods, including beads, utensils, and fabric or blankets, for pelts.

It wasn't until the arrival of Jedediah Strong Smith in 1828 that a white explorer is known to have thoroughly investigated the northern portions of California. He is credited with being the first white man to explore the interior while leading an ambitious two-year trapping expedition from the Great Salt Lake across the Mojave Desert and through the San Bernardino Mountains into central and northern California.

"I wanted to be the first to view a country on which the eyes of a white man had never gazed and to follow the course of rivers that run through a new land," wrote Smith, who spent eight years exploring the West. Indeed, he is credited with being the first white man to enter California overland, the first to cross over the Sierra Nevada, the first to travel the length and breadth of the Great Basin, and the first to travel the California coastline into Oregon.

Having covered an immense area of the West, Smith's party of twenty explorers and trappers (including himself) left Mission San Jose and headed northeast and east. He wrote that on January 1, 1828, they "encamped on Buenaventura River which sometimes is called by the Spaniards the Piscadore." Today we know that they traveled up a branch of the San Joaquin River. In spite of the heavy rain and their relatively impoverished condition, the men trapped forty-five beaver.

After this they traveled north and then northwest, and by mid-April reached the Hay Fork of the Trinity River, where they had several encounters with local tribes. They then journeyed down the South Fork of the Trinity. The terrain was rugged and difficult, especially since they were also driving a heard of three hundred horses and mules over the mountains. Smith's journal reveals that on some days the men managed to advance only one grueling mile and afterwards had to let their exhausted animals rest for several days before pushing on.

On a number of occasions as the party pressed toward the coast, they met Indians who wanted to trade deerskins for axes and knives. Smith reported that many of these Indians had most likely been trading with Hudson's Bay Company trappers, for his men frequently noted evidence of "trees on which axes had been used."

By mid-May it was clear that the men were as exhausted as their animals. Smith wrote that there was little venison to be had and that the weather was bad and "so thick with fog" that it was almost impossible to keep track of the herd of horses.

When the party moved farther west, they encountered forests of spruce, fir, and redwood. Smith described the redwoods as "the noblest trees" he had ever seen. The country, however, was so heavily timbered and brushy, a route through it was almost impossible, and Smith's scouts determined that they would have to backtrack. Smith then went out to scout for himself; he was sadly disappointed to discover their report was true. Heavy fog along the coast slowed their trek once again.

Smith then led his party back to the Klamath River, reaching it on May 24. There they crossed the river, but the men managed to travel downstream only two miles before turning east. Again the countryside proved so treacherous that they had to descend to the river. Once again the fog was so thick that at times the party could not move forward at all. In June they had only traveled a few miles, and Smith wrote, "We have two men, every day that go ahead with axes, to cut a road, and then it is with difficulty we can get along."

There was little game available here, so after killing a dog and rationing out a pint of flour per man, Jedediah killed one of the younger horses. Finally, the party was able to make its way to the ocean and the mouth of Wilson Creek near present-day Requa. Thankfully, Smith managed to kill three elk and the men celebrated.

The party resumed its trek on June 11, and the men had to journey up and down the steep ridges and through the dense redwood forest and heavy brush. On June 14, in the region around Crescent City, travel became easier; they moved along the coastline, even taking to the sea for short stretches to get around some of the rougher points. There was some feed for the horses, and one of the hunters shot a large elk.

On June 20 the party crossed the Smith River (the river that now bears Jedediah's name), and three days later entered what is now Oregon. They reached Oregon's Rogue River on June 27. Sadly, the remainder of the journey would not turn out well for half of Smith's men, who were attacked by a local tribe after separating into two parties on the trek to Fort Vancouver.

Jedediah Smith's journey through this region, however, was significant. It was the door that opened up California and the coastal redwoods to further exploration.

Gold Brings Men and Violence to the Redwood Country

Yet it isn't the gold that I'm wanting
So much as just finding the gold.
It's the great, big, broad land 'way up yonder,
It's the forests where silence has lease;
It's the beauty that thrills me with wonder,
It's the stillness that fills me with peace."
— Robert Service, *The Spell of the*
Yukon and Other Poems

That California is known as the Golden State is no accident. The discovery of gold in 1848 triggered the greatest and most unimaginable mass migration in US history and had a profound impact on the landscape and settlement of California and the West. In 1849 San Francisco's population numbered 2,000. By 1855 it topped 59,000 as more than 300,000 prospectors found their way to California. By 1870 the federal census listed 560,000 Californians.

The rush of miners impacted more than the environment. Mexicans who had dominated the political climate for decades were quickly dispossessed of their power through the influx of Americans and Europeans, while California's native populations were hunted down and murdered or reduced to poverty and life on reservations established to separate them from their land. At the same time, immigrants from all over the world flocked to California, many of them settling in to take up life as townsfolk, farmers, ranchers, and loggers.

Miners flocked to the northern mines on the heels of the discovery of gold in the Sierras.

The gold rush also established San Francisco and Sacramento as cultural, political, economic, and geographic centers. Both cities supplied arriving miners with provisions and attracted bankers and merchants to their growing populations; San Francisco's banking and financial district sits today atop the sunken remains of hundreds of ships abandoned during the heyday of 1849.

Moreover, San Francisco—constructed with wood and heated with wood—rapidly devoured the local stands of oak and smaller pockets of coast redwoods located in the Berkeley Hills canyons. In fact, more than 90 percent of the city's buildings consisted of wood, the highest percentage of any US metropolis. San Francisco burned six times between 1849 and 1851, but each time was rebuilt with more and more regional timber.

A GOLD RUSH IN THE REDWOODS

Most people generally think in terms of the Sierra's Mother Lode when they hear "gold rush," but though the California gold rush may have started at Sutter's Mill, it was the movement into the far north that opened up the vast mountainous and coastal region—including the redwoods—to further exploration and exploitation.

It was after Major P. B. Reading found gold on an unnamed river (which he named Trinity) in 1848 that men rushed into the rugged canyons and mountains of the Klamath, Salmon, and Trinity Rivers. Many traveled south from Oregon, while hordes of hard-luck miners headed north from Sacramento and the Mother Lode, hoping against hope that they'd find more than a little bit of gold dust.

By 1850 whites were also traveling California's northern coastline. Some noticed the glitter of gold along sandy shorelines, and a smattering of beach gold was discovered on the ocean shores in Del Norte County, home of the coastal redwood giants. This brought to Gold Bluff hundreds of miners who believed they could simply pick up handfuls of gold. In truth, few achieved success mining the Gold Bluff's ocean sands—although the dream of easy pickings lured many hopeful argonauts north.

Humboldt Bay, which was first sighted in the early 1800s, was "rediscovered" in 1849 and named in honor of explorer and naturalist Baron

Humboldt Bay and Eureka became important shipping points for supplies coming into the region and for cargo going out.

Alexander von Humboldt. Ultimately the coastal communities of Crescent City, Trinidad, Union (later renamed Arcata), and Eureka became essential ports and shipping points for the myriad supplies headed into the remote and isolated mining camps scattered throughout southern Oregon and northern California. Eureka, founded in 1850, boasted a population of three thousand by 1853. Humboldt Bay would also soon serve as the shipping point for thousands and thousands of board feet of milled redwood lumber.

Ironically, while the thousands of miners tramping through the frigid waters of California's goldfields did not fare well financially or historically, many northern California merchants as well as logging and shipping companies rose quickly to prominence. Even still, as men moved north, into the virgin territories along the coast and inland, most believed they would find their fortunes in the gold mines. Such is the stuff of dreams.

One such party to travel to the coast from the Trinity mines was led by Dr. Josiah Gregg. Gregg and seven men battled the rugged terrain in their quest for gold and finally reached the Pacific Ocean just south of

Trinidad. Though Gregg was interested in more than just mining, his men were impatient to stake out claims and refused to help him with his surveying equipment. He especially wanted to measure the girth of a giant tree, no doubt a redwood, that was presumably twenty-one feet thick. The story is told that the Mad River earned its moniker because the men continued to argue over staying or moving on.

Eventually the group split up, and Gregg and his small party trekked down the Eel River. Not long afterward, Gregg, weakened by hunger and exhaustion, fell from his horse and died, but the remainder of his party traveled on to San Francisco, where news of Trinity and gold spiked immediate interest.

Merchants and land speculators rapidly set out to create a harbor along the coast. Three competing companies arrived at Humboldt Bay within days of each other. Arguing over who had first rights, they finally signed a pact of understanding. One of the parties, under James Talbot Ryan, claimed the eastern shore of the bay. Ryan, an Irishman who became a successful contractor in Boston before heading west to the goldfields, is the man credited with naming and plotting the town that became "Eureka."

"Eureka!" or "I have found it!" became California's famous state motto—however, most people believe the cry is related to James Marshall's initial discovery of gold rather than the discovery of Humboldt Bay. Regardless of which discovery triggered the banner "Eureka!" the race to California was on.

The first miners panned what was easily trapped in the streams. Next, miners joined together to divert water through sluice boxes or long toms, working in small crews. Finally, new methods of mining were developed—methods that ultimately changed California's landscape and environment, including the entire redwood coast. The most devastating enterprise involved hydraulic mining, which grew rapidly in popularity so that by 1860 it was the dominant technology, employing hundreds of men.

Bayard Taylor's *New Pictures from California*, first published in 1852, described how these hydraulic operations—with high-pressure hoses known as "giants"—blasted water at hillsides at 120 pounds of pressure per square inch in order to release the buried gold, "like a giant bleeding to death from a single vein—the mountain washed itself away."

Some better-known gold mines in Humboldt County included the Red Cap Mine, located north of Eureka, as well as the Big Bar Annex Placer Mine, the Cavanaugh Mine, the China Flat Placer Mine, the Bissel Mine, the Coleman Placer Mine, the Delaney Group of Mines, the Harveston Bar Mine, and the Prospect Hill Mine.

Though less famous than the mines in the Sierras, these were the catalysts that brought more and more settlers into northern California and southern Oregon, and they were the driving force that brought men to discover the redwood forests lining the coastline.

The rush also brought violence and bloodshed to the tribes who resided here, and in response to this assault, the federal government sent Reddick McKee to begin treaty negotiations. His expedition traveled throughout the northern reaches of California, meeting with tribal leaders and making treaties, and, at the same time, recording historic and important ethnographic information. It's hard not to consider this information a bird's-eye view of life in the region at the time of the gold rush.

George Gibbs's Journal of the Reddick McKee Expedition

George Gibbs was born in New York in 1815 and died in 1873. He graduated from Harvard University with a degree in law in 1838 and started a legal practice. However, the law did not appeal to him, and when the opportunity arose to go west, which had only just come under American control, he moved to Oregon with the Mounted Rifle Regiment. In Oregon he was appointed deputy customs collector at Astoria and later became attached to Oregon's Indian Commission, where he learned the Chinook language.

What year Gibbs came to California is not known, but in July 1851 he was in Sonoma, where he joined McKee's expedition. In 1852 Gibbs returned to northern California as a gold miner. He then wrote his *Observations on the Indians of the Klamath River and Humboldt Bay, Accompanying Vocabularies of Their Languages*, which was published in 1853. The document has become one of the most important early accounts of the physical nature of the region as well as observations on the region's Native American cultures.

Gibbs's journal was written in 1851 while he served as interpreter on the expedition led by US Indian agent Reddick McKee. McKee had been appointed as one of three treaty commissioners by President Millard Fillmore and sent into the Coast Ranges north of San Francisco Bay as well as portions of northern California, which lay beyond the area assigned to O. M. Wozencraft. McKee made four treaties with California's northernmost tribes, the ones officially referred to as O, P, Q, and R.

One important aspect of Gibbs's journal is that, according to Pliny Goddard, "the first mention of the Chilula is by George Gibbs, who passed directly through the territory in 1851." Gibbs wrote of the Chilula: "Of the Indians of Redwood Creek, called by the Whites Bald Hills Indians, little was learned, and none of them could be induced to come in. They were termed *Oruk* by the Coast Indians, and *Tcho-lo-lah* by the *Weits-peks*. The general opinion is, that they are more nearly allied to the Trinity than to the Klamath tribes. The names of some of their bands, as given by an Indian, were, commencing at the coast, the *Cherr-h-quuh*, *Ot-teh-petl*, *Oh-nah*, *Oh-pah* and *Roque-Choh*."

In addition to writing about the expedition's encounters with various tribes, Gibbs described the terrain and the topography. He also made pencil sketches of scenes along the route, which were reproduced for the public as well.

From August to September, Gibbs wrote about the expedition's trek through northern California, describing the redwoods and the landscape in detail. In early September the party made camp. This is how Gibbs described their location:

> *The last part of our march led us into a thick redwood forest, upon a mountain, through which we were obliged to cut our trail, the ground being covered with under-brush and fallen timber. A fatiguing climb and an excessively bad descent brought us again to the South Fork. On the other side was a small prairie of about eighty acres, from which, however, the grass was mostly burnt, a bare sufficiency only remaining. As it was already evening, and the march had been the most laborious we had yet made, we had no opportunity of seeking further. It had drizzled a good part of the day, and the night was still wet.*

. . . Our camp was a very pretty one, the little prairie being level and rich, and encircled by a magnificent redwood forest. One tree near the tents I measured, and found it to be fifty-two feet in circumference, at four or five feet from the ground, and this although the bark and a portion of the wood were burned away. It was still erect and alive at the top, notwithstanding the interior had been hollowed out to the height of probably eighty feet, and the smoke was even yet escaping from a hole in the side.

The diameter, measured through a chasm at the bottom, was eighteen feet. Another, likewise much burnt, measured forty-nine feet in circumference, at five feet from the ground. The stump of a group rising from one root was twenty-two feet ten inches across. Those above mentioned were single trees, and without swell, the measurements given being the fair size of the shaft. Colonel M'Kee measured a fallen trunk near camp, which was three hundred and twenty-five feet in length, though not of extraordinary thickness. Larger trees than this are known to exist, but none were noticed by ourselves. Their shafts, often disposed in groups, rise to a vast height free from limbs, and their foliage is delicate and feathery. The bark is of an ash color, very thick, but not rough; the branches are small in proportion, and the leaves resemble those of the hemlock rather than the cedar. The wood, however, is like that of the latter tree, and of a red color. It splits very readily, so much so, that the Indians, without the use of iron, get out immense planks for their huts. In a manufactured state, it is unsurpassed for shingles, ceiling, and weather boarding. The redwood appears to belong exclusively to the coast region; nowhere, it is believed, at least in northern California, extending inland more than twenty-five or thirty miles, and it does not reach a more northern latitude than the parallel of 42 [degrees].

Likewise, on September 17, Gibbs described their arrival at Humboldt "City" and Humboldt Bay:

To-day the camp was broken up, and we moved down to "Humboldt City." The road, for the grater [sic] part of the distance, ran over hills covered with low brush. It is passable for wagons from the settlement near Van Dusen's fork, to an embarcadero on a slough putting up from the bay, whence produce is taken by water. The town, if it may be called so, is situated upon a little plateau of about forty acres, nearly opposite the entrance, and under a bluff, rising from the midst of a tract of low ground. It contains only about a dozen houses, and was at this time nearly deserted; Uniontown, at the head of the bay, [has] proved a more successful rival in the packing trade. Vessels of considerable size can lie close to the shore here; but the place is not destined to any importance, at least until the settlement and cultivation of the adjoining country shall make it a point of export for provisions.

Gibbs's entry on September 24 describes the terrain, including the area of Redwood Creek and the Bald Hills:

Some fifteen or twenty miles from the coast, the redwood timber disappears, and oak-covered hills extend back to the foot of the mountains, affording good pasturage, and some farming land. The immediate bottom of the river is narrow, and covered with alder and balm of Gilead. At this time it was about thirty or forty feet across, and knee-deep to our horses; but in winter it swells to sixty or seventy yards in width. The Humboldt trail to the Trinity crosses it some fifteen miles farther up. Leaving the river, we ascended a long spur of mountain to the top of the dividing ridge between it and Redwood creek, through alternate forest and prairie land. The character of the mountains, from this to the Klamath, differs widely from those we had before passed over. Their summits are broader, and the declivities less steep and broken. Prairies of rich grass lie on their southern slopes, and especially on their tops, from whence their name of Bald Hills is derived. This grass was now yellow with ripeness, and the wind, sweeping over its long slender stems, gave it a beautiful appearance. The Indians use the stalks in their finer basket-work; and, when split, in the braids with which they tie up their hair, and other ornamental fabrics. The timber here becomes much more open, and fir, white and yellow, predominates over the redwood. This last is now chiefly confined to the immediate neighborhood of the coast. Springs of good water occur near almost all these prairies, and camps are therefore selected on their skirts. Late in the season, however, the grass is often burned, and dependence cannot always be placed upon the usual grounds. In winter, snow lies on them for several weeks, and to a considerable depth. Elk are very abundant in these mountains, and the ground was marked everywhere with their footprints.

From September 29 until October 9, 1851, Reddick's expedition made camp at the junction of the Klamath and Trinity Rivers. During that time, Gibbs gathered information and provided detailed descriptions of the tribes with whom they came into contact. For example, he wrote:

The lodges of these Indians are generally very well built; being made of boards from the redwood or fir, and of considerable size, often reaching twenty feet square. The roofs are pitched over a ridgepole, and sloping each way; the ground being unusually excavated to the depth of three or four feet, and a pavement of smooth stones laid in front. The cellars of the better class are also floored and walled with stone. The door always consists of a round hole in a heavy plank, just sufficient to admit the body; and is formed with a view to exclude the bears, who in winter make occasional and very unwelcome visits.

CLASHES WITH NATIVE AMERICANS

Interestingly, of all of the 117 tribes who called California home, the Karuk, Yurok, and Hupa were the last to meet up with the white wave sweeping through the region. However, like all other California tribes, these tribes barely survived the onslaught of white settlement, attack, and disease.

Hostilities, of course, grew as whites moved in and through traditional territories. The Chilula resented the pack trains that came more and more frequently into their land.

Although the Chilula kept the whites from their land for a time, fear among the white settlers grew. Town meetings were held as to how to handle the "Indian problem."

Finally, action was taken to trap the Chilula and remove them, but still not satisfied, volunteers banded together to take on the tribes, an action that the officers of the army refused to take. In effect, the Chilula, whose numbers did not exceed six hundred at the time of contact, were nearly decimated.

According to Rosa A. Palmer in *The North American Indians: An Account of the American Indians North of Mexico*, "The remaining families, with the exception of one or two, moved to Hupa Valley. On the reservation they gradually lost distinctiveness of their language and fell into the ways of the Hupa. As a separate people, the Chilula no longer exists."

Likewise, the Tolowa barely survived as a tribe after three massacres in each of the years 1853 through 1855 while gathered for their World Renewal Ceremonies. In 1853 the vigilantes attacked—as the people danced. As retold in *Genocide in Northwestern California*: "The whites attacked and the bullets were everywhere. Over four hundred and fifty of our people were murdered or lay dying on the ground. Then the whitemen built a huge fire and threw in our sacred ceremonial dresses, the regalia, and our feathers, and the flames grew higher. Then they threw in the babies, many of them were still alive. Some tied weights around the necks of the dead and threw them into the water."

Such violence is hard for anyone today to comprehend. Though many settlers tried to protect various tribespeople, the violence was hard to contain—even by the army.

It was as if the silence of the redwoods had been shattered forever.

In addition to the increasing violence, forced labor was widespread, even legitimized by the Act for the Government and Protection of Indians, enacted in 1850. Between 1850 and 1863 perhaps as many as ten thousand Indians were indentured—in particular, females until age fifteen and males until age eighteen. Moreover, in the case of offences committed by whites, justice was absent. No white man was held accountable. The system was, in effect, a localized form of slavery.

While Indian retaliation and resistance were common, the result was only more bloodshed. Historic estimates of the Yurok population vary slightly, but Alfred L. Kroeber in 1925 estimated that the 1770 population probably numbered 2,500; by 1870 it had declined to 1,350, and by 1910 the Yurok reportedly numbered only 668 to 700 individuals.

Kroeber also estimated that the 1770 Wiyot population had originally reached 1,000, while Sherburne Cook, who wrote during the 1920s and '30s, suggested their numbers likely totaled 1,500. He later revised that estimate up to 3,300.

Tragically, the Wiyot were massacred on February 26, 1860, by Captain Seman Wright and his vigilantes, who vowed to "to kill every peaceable Indian—man, woman, and child." Calling themselves the "Humboldt Volunteers, Second Brigade," it was Fort Humboldt's commander at this time, Gabriel Rains, who reported to his commanding officer that Wright and his men had organized themselves at Hydesville and Eel River (now named Rohnerville) and were determined to annihilate the Wiyot.

Bret Harte, working as a printer's helper and assistant editor at a local newspaper, the *Northern Californian*, documented the Indian Island

Bret Harte, journalist and writer, revealed much about life in the early mining days.
PHOTO COURTESY FORT JONES MUSEUM

Massacre in a scathing editorial. He wrote, "A more shocking and revolting spectacle never was exhibited to the eyes of a Christian and civilized people."

Although Harte's journalistic reporting raised eyebrows, it also raised protests, and the publisher asked Harte to leave.

Without a doubt, tribal populations were decimated, targeted by miners searching for gold and later by settlers taking up homesteads inside the Redwood Belt, especially after the Homestead Act of 1862 spurred even more settlement across the West. The period from 1850 until the 1870s was a time of great violence and sadness as tribes, their lands, and their sacred sites in and around the forests were overrun.

As noted by one Karuk elder, "*Yis-ara-to-peen*, new people are taking over."

By the end of the gold rush "era," at least 75 percent of the Yurok were eliminated, either from massacre or diseases brought in with the surge of white miners, and the Tolowa's, Chilula's, Wiyot's, and Karuk's numbers were equally reduced.

In fact, of the approximately 200,000-plus Native Americans residing in California at contact, only 15,500 survived into the 1900s. One reporter noted in the *Humboldt Times*, "If [the Indians] resisted, they were killed, butchered, shot down with as little hesitation as wolves and coyotes."

In truth, the magnificent redwoods were running red with the blood of thousands.

FORT HUMBOLDT, BUILT TO PROTECT SETTLERS AND TRIBES

Fort Humboldt is now a California State Historic Park. It was built to protect both settlers and tribes. As conditions between miners and settlers and the local tribes deteriorated during the gold rush, the army established the fort in northern California. It was clear that soldiers stationed at Fort Jones, some 150 miles to the northeast, and Fort Reading, about 150 miles to the east, could not halt the growing violence.

Conditions for soldiers at the time were rough and spare. The 4th Infantry, ordered to the new fort, sustained over a hundred deaths due to cholera after journeying from the Great Lakes, down the Atlantic Ocean routes, across Panama, and up the Pacific coast to San Francisco.

To establish the new fort, the army chose two companies of the 4th Infantry under Captain and Brevet Lieutenant Colonel Robert C. Buchanan. After serving twenty-two years in the army, Buchanan was given the "privilege" of selecting the site for the new fort. He named it Fort Humboldt and immediately set his troops to work building the quarters and stockade that would serve them.

At its peak, the fort maintained fourteen buildings, all of crude plank construction. It was laid out in typical military fashion, with a "parade square" at the center. Along with two buildings that served as barracks for the enlisted men, there were quarters for the officers, an office, a hospital, a bakery, a storehouse/commissary, a guardhouse, a blacksmith shop, and a stable.

The fort remained active from 1853 to 1870 and was responsible for trying to halt the number of depredations and vigilante attacks on Indians while trying to protect settlers. Among the well-known soldiers who served at Fort Humboldt were young Captain Ulysses S. Grant, who served for five months in 1853–54; Robert C. Buchanan, who became a general during the Civil War; Charles S. Lovell, who would command a brigade during the Second Battle of Bull Run, Antietam, and Fredericksburg; George Crook, who also became a general during the Civil War; Gabriel J. Rains, who later became a brigadier general in the Confederate army; and Dr. Lafayette Guild, who would serve directly under General Robert E. Lee.

Fort Humboldt was registered as a California Historical Landmark on January 11, 1935, and designated a State Historic Park in 1963.

Logging: How the Redwoods
Became a Source of Wealth

From the early days of European migration to America, in the 17th Century, the prototype of buildings was based on English precedent, even if mostly translated into the locally available material in abundance: timber.

— HARRY SEIDLER, ARCHITECT, 1923–2006

As penned by John C. Merriam, "When one looks at one of these immense trees and then at the man with his small axe and saw, he is quite inclined to believe in the story of the man who chopped a week on one side before he discovered that another man had been working eight days on the other side of the same tree."

Such is the size of a coastal redwood!

Before the gold rush, only a few early immigrants in California harvested redwood for timber, primarily around the Santa Cruz Mountains. Under Mexico's rule, the principal industries in California included cattle and tallow. There was little interest in timber. These early loggers felled trees with axes and then shaped the logs into beams to be dragged to a sawpit and cut into planks. Because of its scarcity, this finished lumber could bring in as much as $50 per thousand board feet, meaning that a skilled sawyer could earn about $2 to $3 a day, a good sum for the time. Mission Indians did much of the manual labor.

But milling redwoods was a fairly difficult task prior to the gold rush and settlement eras, so that, for the most part, the massive trees were left alone.

This redwood stump is estimated to be 2,500 years old,
based on the diameter of its trunk.

One man credited with bringing redwood to light in the pre–gold
rush days, however, was Thomas O. Larkin, an American immigrant who
arrived in California in 1832. By the 1840s he was exporting redwood
boards, doors, window frames, and shingles to ports around the world,
including Hawaii and Tahiti. In 1846 alone, Larkin reportedly shipped a

million board feet to be sold in the eastern United States. Of course, with news of the gold strike in 1848, loggers working for Larkin and other lumbermen rushed off to the Sierras. As a result, the supply of lumber dropped even as the demand for timber increased.

E. C. Williams, one of the first men to pursue the commercial value of redwood, reminisced in 1912 about his journey through the redwood wilderness in the spring of 1850. Traveling up the Big River in a rough redwood canoe, he noted "[the river's] slight ripples meeting the verdure of the shore, the tall redwoods with their great symmetrical trunks traveling toward the skies; with the bright colors of the rhododendrons profusely scattered in the placid river and over all the hush and solitude of the primeval forest—all combining to impress upon our minds the beauty and truth [in] Bryant's *Thanatopsis*, 'The groves were God's first temples.'"

In retrospect, Williams also wrote, "I cannot but regret the part it appeared necessary for me to enact in what now looks like a desecration."

Logging, however, followed closely on the heels of mining. There was a need to fuel the boilers used at the mines to separate the gold, and wood was needed for the flumes that carried water to the mining sites. Hard-rock miners with pickaxes dug shafts as deep as forty feet or more, while thousands of miles of tunnels were either dug out or blasted out of the area's rich mountainsides—all requiring timber to shore them up. Most mining companies thus became logging companies as well, setting up sawmills alongside their stamp mills and other operations.

Because the first sawmills were not equipped to deal with the size of the redwood trees, however, and because early lumbermen were more familiar with the kinds of trees they'd milled in the East—in particular, pine, spruce, and fir—it was almost five years before the coast redwoods were seen as a real commodity and logged.

In 1851 logging began in earnest. The redwood—still a relatively unknown tree to easterners—was not the major timber product, and because California's northernmost region had remained outside the influence of the Mexican government, its great stands of redwoods were virtually virgin territory. Within five years, however, the redwood's size and value, especially its ability to withstand weather, warping, or twisting, would transform it into an alternative source of "gold."

Harry Meiggs, an alderman in San Francisco, owned a pier near the now-famous Fisherman's Wharf. After hearing that a ship from the Orient had run aground off the Mendocino coast, he sent a crew to salvage what he thought would be a rich cargo of silk. Instead his men discovered trees so tall and broad that twenty men standing hand-to-hand could not encircle one of them.

Meiggs knew a gold mine when he saw it. He set up a sawmill near Mendocino and quickly set to work, shipping load after load of redwood lumber back to the young and eager San Francisco. Though Meiggs later fled to South America under a cloud of debt and speculation, it can be said that he set off the coastal redwood boom that would span more than a century.

The first lumber mill operating in Del Norte County was a small mill built in Crescent City by F. E. Weston in 1853. Logs were hauled in on two large wheels twelve feet in diameter. The first large mill was located on Lake Earl, north of Crescent City; built in 1873 by several local businessmen, it was later sold to outside interests.

Next, Hobbs, Wall & Company built another mill at Crescent City and soon built a railroad from town to their timber site. The railroad was then incorporated as the Crescent City & Smith River Railroad and, by 1889, the company had finished construction of a bridge over the Smith River. This allowed for passenger trains to run to the town of Smith River. Eventually Hobbs, Wall & Company became the only large mill operator in the county, and, while plans were made to expand the use of rails, the proposal to connect to the port city of Crescent City was never realized and the company removed the rails in the northern portion of Del Norte County.

In 1913 the Brookings Timber & Lumber Company began work on a large sawmill, and the community of Brookings was laid out across the Chetco River. However, because their operation only shipped fir, it was soon floundering. A group of timbermen, who were operating under the title of the Del Norte Company, approached the Brookings Company with an offer. The result: In January 1916 the California & Oregon Lumber Company was formed, capital was raised to the tune of $5 million, and the company made the switch from fir to redwood.

In 1922 the first redwood trees were cut on Rowdy Creek, located east of the town of Smith River. Unfortunately, the operation again floundered and profits dipped. By the summer of 1925, the mill cut its last redwood log.

Although Del Norte County and, farther south, Mendocino County were redwood-producing counties, it was Humboldt County—home of today's Redwood National Park—that became the most significant region for harvesting redwood. Its forest reserves yielded a greater percentage of clear timber. Out of an approximate land area of 2,224,000 acres, it was estimated that more than 1,000,000 acres were forested, and out of that were at least 538,000 acres of redwoods. Because of the quality of the redwoods located in Humboldt County, the area was recognized as the "heart" of the California Redwood Belt.

The very first sawmill on Humboldt Bay was built by Martin White and James Eddy. Their mill, the Taupoos, was founded in September

Humboldt County became the heart of the Redwood Belt.

1850 and sat near what is now Second and M Streets in Eureka. Unfortunately it failed within the first year.

William Carson, who started his lumber career working for Ryan & Duff, soon left to purchase the Hula Mill in 1854. A visionary and entrepreneur with extravagant tastes, Carson is credited with bringing the first ox team to Humboldt County in addition to constructing the most elaborate and ornate Victorian mansion in Eureka. Built entirely out of redwood, even today the Carson Mansion is considered one of the most beautiful examples of Victorian architecture in the West.

Rather than trying to mill the larger redwoods, however, William Carson selected smaller logs to mill, enabling him to successfully ship twenty thousand board feet of redwood lumber to San Francisco. Meanwhile, Harry Meiggs's old partners, in an effort to recoup their losses after he fled to South America, set up two redwood mills. Unfortunately mill fires, shipwrecks, and floods and fires in the woods, along with fluctuating prices, made lumbering a risky enterprise for several years.

Even still, San Franciscans fell in love with redwood.

The properties of redwood quickly made it the "wood of choice" up and down California. In general, redwood's grain is very straight, making it easier to cut and trim into planks or work into carvings and moldings. In addition, there is far less shrinkage when drying, so that once seasoned, redwood is rarely affected by climate or weather. This made it ideal for the flumes miners were building to transfer water from rivers and creeks. And as railroad ties, redwood timbers far exceeded pine in their ability to withstand weather and time. Since hundreds of miles of railroads were being constructed along the Pacific coast, redwood ties were always in demand.

Redwood shingles became another important commodity as the industry took off; the lack of resin in redwood shingles made them more tolerant and less susceptible to fire and decay. Sadly, of course, though much of San Francisco was built with redwood siding and shingles, it did not halt the city's burning following the catastrophic 1906 earthquake.

Redwood water tanks and vats were also popular; as storage tanks for breweries, redwood became more popular than oak, which had always been the wood preferred by brewers. A layer of shellac was applied to the interior of the redwood staves, and that prevented any interaction with the contents. Railroad companies, such as the Southern Pacific and Central Pacific, used redwood in the construction of their water tanks positioned up and down their lines. And tanneries found redwood superior to other woods in the construction of their vats.

Finally, redwood stave pipes, used in piping water for domestic, agricultural, and other uses, became popular. The staves were tightly pressed together by steel hoops and joined with steel plates.

By 1900 even California's architects were responding to this love of redwood. Under the influence of Reverend Joseph Worcester, regional architects began using natural redwood for both the interiors and the exteriors of their homes. Bernard Maybeck used redwood shingles on the exteriors of his houses while finishing the interiors with natural redwood. The emerging "California bungalow" style was, in fact, a merging of the architecture of the English bungalow and the California adobe. And these homes were built entirely of redwood.

Clearly, the demand for these magnificent trees was not about to subside; in fact, as noted in the *San Francisco Call* in November 1895, "The commercial value of these trees has been steadily growing, and in spite of the protests of the lovers of nature the demand has been met with a ready supply. A wood that will not rot, is hard to burn, easy to work up, of a rich mahogany color and not difficult to procure, holds out too many inviting inducements to expect any mercy from the human race."

With such demand, logging companies sprung up everywhere across northern California, particularly along the coast, and as they did, their manner of operation also underwent changes. New methods of milling had to be engineered to accommodate the redwood's immense size; the average redwood exceeded the norm by many feet, some reaching fifteen or twenty feet, or more, in diameter. Mills traditionally used for sawing pine were only capable of milling logs with a diameter of eight or ten feet at best.

In the early days, logging around Humboldt Bay was facilitated by the slope of the land towards the bay. The bay served as a natural "log pond" where logs were easily transported to the nearby mills onshore.

The introduction of steam power radically transformed the entire lumber industry but, most importantly, the redwood industry. The first

The size of redwoods forced mills to change their operations to accommodate the size of redwood logs.

steam train built in California in the 1850s was used to haul redwood logs and lumber from the area's forests and mills to Arcata, located on Humboldt Bay. It was a tramway six miles long with cars drawn by a steam donkey. Soon that small tramway matured into more than a hundred miles of railroad track linking the woods to the mills and the mills to Humboldt Bay's shipping docks.

That soon changed, and the single biggest factor in the expansion of lumber mills was the railroad. Railroads, of a more primitive nature,

The Timber Heritage Association

The Timber Heritage Association (THA) is a volunteer-based group whose goal is to raise awareness and develop appreciation for the history of timber, logging, and railroads in Humboldt County. The group originated when a handful of individuals joined together in 1977 to help preserve the local timber and railroad history. Initially the group was called the Northern Counties Logging and Interpretive Association and their principal activity was to help with the logging exhibit at Fort Humboldt State Historic Park in Eureka.

Not long after, they realized that historic logging/timber/railroad artifacts were quickly disappearing or falling into ruin. To that end, the association managed to restore a steam donkey, Bear Harbor Lumber Co. locomotive No. 1, and Elk River Mill & Lumber Co. locomotive No. 1; the group then began sharing the restored engines locally as well as at rail fairs and logging conferences.

Hoping to generate interest and funds in developing a state rail museum, the association was disappointed when it became clear that there were no state park funds available to make it happen. That's when the association decided it would have to pursue the means to make it happen, and the concept of a Timber Heritage Museum was born.

In 2004 the organization changed its name to the Timber Heritage Association, and, although the group continues to support the logging exhibit at Fort Humboldt State Park, it is planning to develop a separate museum as well as an excursion train that would

appeared in the California redwoods as early as 1852: Mules and oxen would pull log cars over rails that had been shaped from tracks of timber. These rails could be laid or moved according to the needs of the logging crews.

The first railroads appeared in Humboldt County in 1854. By the end of 1854, there were more than twenty miles of well-constructed railroads built by loggers.

No doubt, completion of the first transcontinental railroad in 1869 was a boon to those who dreamed of linking one station to the next up and down California. For most people, travel meant riding in wagons or travel around Humboldt Bay. The association has pursued grants as well as donations to keep the dream alive.

After several failed attempts to find storage for the thousands of artifacts the group had collected, the 115-year-old former Hammond Lumber Company roundhouse and shops, located in Samoa, became available for short-term lease. With 7,025 square feet of new roofing on the old roundhouse, the enormous building is now home to six locomotives. The site is not only perfect for the trains stored there, but its own history is fascinating and important. The roundhouse was built in 1893, and out of more than ten thousand roundhouses once located along California's coastline, there are only four left. The roundhouse at Samoa is the oldest.

According to Mike Kellogg, one of Timber Heritage Association's members and active volunteers, "Until 1922, there was no road into Samoa. Anyone hoping to come to Samoa had to take a ferry from Eureka, so everything the men needed, they either manufactured or had to wait until it could be shipped in."

He added that in 1910, the Hammond Lumber Company's own machine crew built a whole locomotive, something no other lumber company had ever managed to do. Mike again pointed out, "The skill involved in such an undertaking is hard to appreciate, but it only goes to show how highly skilled these men were."

In time it is the association's hope that enough donations will come in to realize the dream of a museum that can protect and share the artifacts, photographs, and other memorabilia that played such a prominent role in northern California and redwood history.

stages over rough, crude roads, so the notion of riding the rails had to thrill anyone.

One project that thrilled eager entrepreneurs was the proposal for a railroad to be built from Sausalito to Humboldt Bay—a distance of nearly three hundred miles. Preliminary surveys were made through Marin and Sonoma Counties, and on July 4, 1868, the groundbreaking for the proposed San Francisco and Humboldt Bay Railroad took place near Petaluma. Unfortunately it quickly became clear that the cost of construction was more than expected, and the idea was scrapped in 1869.

While there were only nine sawmills in Eureka in 1854, according to an early report published by the Redwood Lumber Manufacturers Association, twenty-six major redwood mills were built around Humboldt Bay by 1897. In addition, at least twenty-five mills were manufacturing redwood shingles and shakes, while a handful of other mills began manufacturing doors, windowsills, and moldings. The railroads enabled companies to move away from the bay, closer to their source of timber, and allowed mills to log areas farther away from the streambeds.

One of the first small railroad lines to impact the industry was the Arcata and Mad River Railroad. Its first line opened in 1881 as a narrow-gauge road, 12.9 miles long. Interestingly, the Simpson Timber Company used this same line well into the next century; it moved finished lumber from Korbel to the mail line of the Northwestern Pacific at Korblex near Arcata. In addition, a number of mills relied on these small railroads to move their logs and/or lumber.

Within a few years, logging in the region was producing about 150,000,000 board feet in lumber exports annually, and most of it was loaded onto schooners docked at Humboldt Bay. In 1876 alone, 1,100 ships arrived to line up at the docks and take on twenty million board feet of redwood. Some of these vessels sailed to the islands of the Pacific, Australia, and even China.

Railroads soon became the means of hauling logs to the mills.

Arcata's two-mile wharf was one of the longest wharves in the United States, and the Union Plank Walk Rail Track, built by the Union Plank Walk Rail Track and Wharf Company in 1855, ran the entire length of the wharf to where August Jacoby's storehouse sat on the southwest corner of the plaza. Later the rail track became part of the Arcata and Mad River Railroad.

To load such quantities of lumber onto the ships docked on the bay, a system of chutes was constructed that reached from the nearby bluffs above the harbor to the ships below, where seamen removed the milled lumber piece by piece.

Though redwood became the area's dominant resource, the other wood being cut in significant quantities in Humboldt County was pine and fir. Douglas fir was used for shipbuilding, an industry that became nearly as important as the redwood mills themselves. The four-masted *Jane L. Stanford*, for example—the largest wooden vessel to be built in California at this time—was launched on Humboldt Bay, built with Douglas fir. Without such stout schooners, the logging companies would not have been able to market their redwood worldwide.

A few of Humboldt County's early redwood mills included the Elk River Mill, the Samoa Mill, the Union Mill, the Occidental Mill, and the Eel River Valley Lumber Company's and the Milford Land and Lumber Company's mills. The most important mill, however, had to be the Scotia Mill, located outside of today's RNSP, constructed by the Pacific Lumber Company (later known as PL), on the Eel River.

The Pacific Lumber Company was established in 1869; though they controlled ten thousand acres in the Scotia area until 1881, they had not yet begun to log the area. In 1882 a new company was formed—having retained the same name—whose directors were searching for an outlet for its lumber. As a result, the company decided to build a railroad from Forestville to Humboldt Bay, twenty-three miles north. In that same year, two things occurred that changed their fortunes: 1) the company incorporated the Humboldt Bay and Eel River Railroad; and 2) Charles Heney deeded to PL his right-of-way to his landing on the southwest corner of Humboldt Bay. PL also purchased land at Fields Landing to build a port from which its ships would set sail.

Meanwhile, John Vance, William Carson, H. H. Buhne, J. W. Henderson, and others incorporated the Eel River and Eureka Railroad (ER&ERR) in November of 1882. The new line opened for business between Fields Landing and Hydesville in November 1884, and was completed to Eureka in July 1885. John Vance bought the controlling interest in 1886.

Pacific Lumber's line was also completed in 1885 and connected with the ER&ERR at Alton. The mill at Forestville was in operation, and no less than 150 men were now working in the mill and in the woods.

Afraid that Pacific Lumber would run too much competition if its railroad construction was extended, John Vance and William Carson offered to charge PL one dollar for each thousand board feet that their line, the ER&ERR, hauled from Alton to Fields Landing. Pacific Lumber accepted the deal, and the ER&ERR took PL's lumber to the wharf at Fields Landing. The company then turned its attention to the south.

Unfortunately fire destroyed the Pacific Lumber mill in 1895, although construction on a new, bigger mill began right away.

The Scotia Mill, built by Pacific Lumber, soon became the largest mill in the Humboldt Redwood Belt.

FRANK PATTERSON, PHOTOGRAPHER

PL's Scotia Mill, built in July 1897, became the largest mill in the Humboldt Redwood Belt, having a capacity output of 135,000 board feet per day. It boasted three band saws, along with a band splitter, a gang saw, and two gang edgers. It was considered a "complete" mill and far outshone other mills in the region.

Pacific Lumber's timber holdings also comprised some of the finest stands of redwood in the region. The company constructed railroads, over which redwood logs were hauled to the mill and its finished lumber hauled to the company's wharf at Field's Landing on South Bay—an arm of Humboldt Bay. The company also owned its own vessels, which transported its finished product to ports worldwide.

The Samoa Mill was another "newer" and more sophisticated mill for its time (built circa 1895), constructed by the John Vance Mill and Lumber Company. Located on Humboldt Bay, it boasted an elevated tramway over which lumber was moved from the mill out on the wharf to be dropped immediately into push cars and transported to waiting vessels. A crane that moved up and down the track unloaded the lumber into the ships' holds.

The logs for the Samoa Mill were cut on the company's redwood property located on the Mad River and Lindsay Creek and were hauled by railroad twelve to fifteen miles to the mill site. The Vance Lumber Company also owned some of the finest timber in the region, known for its clear grain. It owned three ships and was the principal supplier to Australia.

Prior to being bought up by the Samoa Land and Improvement Company in 1889, Samoa was known as Brownsville, named for a dairy farmer, James Henry Brown, who settled in Humboldt in 1865. Brown was the first permanent white settler to make a home on the north peninsula of Humboldt Bay. The Samoa Land and Improvement Company sold out to the Vance Lumber Company in 1892, and the Samoa lumber mill quickly grew to become the largest in Humboldt County after it was sold to Andrew B. Hammond in 1900. In 1909 the company was reorganized as the Hammond Lumber Company. During World War I it became a shipyard, where seven large wooden steamships were built.

Jim Timmons, born in 1926, was a second-generation sheep and cattle rancher. He related what life was like living on the ranch worked

Timber Company Towns

During the heyday of the logging era, many timber companies established their own "towns." The towns served the mill, and the mill provided the services every family needed; until recently, many of these company towns were still in operation. A few of the most notable company towns in the region included Cranell (Bullwinkle), Korbel (North Fork), Samoa (West Eureka), Scotia (Forestville), Newburg, Falk, and Metropolitan.

In 1869 the Pacific Lumber Company was incorporated, and in 1882 logging began. The town of Forestville was established, but the name was later changed to Scotia so as to avoid confusion with a town in Sonoma that had the same name. PL was, of course, one of the largest producers of lumber in the area. Sadly, the company was the victim of a "hostile" takeover in 1986. When the new company filed bankruptcy in 2008, it was sold to Humboldt Redwood Company, and the town was sold to another company.

In 1882 the Eel River Valley Lumber Company purchased a redwood stand near Fortuna. The mill was built in 1884; a town,

by his father, which supplied food for the Hammond Lumber Company's Samoa cookhouse and the men who worked up at the "wood camps."

From *Humboldt Heartland*, a series of memoirs collected by Andy Westfall, Timmons wrote:

When I was little there were still three logging camps active in Little River and up behind Big Lagoon. At that time there was a cookhouse and cabins for the single men and several houses for the married men. There were at least nine full time employees working in the ranch department and in summertime, with haying and all the different activities going on, why there were probably over 20 people that worked here. . . . The ranch had a lot of beef cattle and the cattle ran in the cutover land. Up at Little River is where the cattle were kept. We spent a lotta time up around a place called Camp 20 about 7 miles up Little River. It was the Hammond family camp before the Hammond dubbed Newburg, was established and included twenty houses, twenty-five cabins, and a store. In 1931 the mill shut down due to the Depression and was dismantled in 1943.

Korbel was established circa 1882 as North Fork, but the name was changed to Korbel in 1891. The Korbel Brothers, vineyard owners from Sonoma, sold out to the Northern Redwood Company in 1913. The company was again sold in 1956 to the Simpson Redwood Company. The town began to decline in the 1930s; few houses are left today, but those are still owned by the company.

Samoa, the company town, is today a historic community. Located on the peninsula across from Eureka, John Vance Mill and Lumber Company built a large complex here after a fire burned the original mill in 1892. With no roads into Samoa, access was by boat, making a town necessary (at this time it was not a company town). A. B. Hammond purchased the town and mill in 1900, and he later bought up the privately owned houses, thus making it a company town. Georgia Pacific purchased the property in 1956, but it was turned over to Louisiana Pacific in 1972, followed by Simpson Timber and other companies.

Company bought out Little River Redwood Company and moved the whole operation to Crannell.

As a side note: The Georgia-Pacific Corporation purchased the Samoa complex in 1956 and built a plywood mill in 1958. In 1964 a modernized sawmill replaced the original mill. Some of the older homes, built for its employees, were razed during the remodeling, but the Samoa Cookhouse was preserved. Today it is open to the public, serving meals as well as providing a museum.

The Samoa mill complex was eventually transferred to the Louisiana-Pacific Corporation in 1972. The last old growth redwood was milled in 1980.

Another Mad River mill was the Riverside Mill, located on the bank of the river about a mile from the fork of the North Fork. The timber owned by this company was considered some of the finest in the area.

The Riverside Lumber Company, owned by H. W. Jackson of Arcata, collected its redwood logs in an immense pond. To move the lumber from the mill to the company's Arcata shipping docks, the Arcata and Mad River Railroad Company built a switch track, over which the finished lumber was hauled eleven miles.

The North Fork Mill was also located on the Mad River, twelve miles east of Arcata, at the site of the small town of Korbel. The mill was operated by the Humboldt Lumber Milling Company and owned principally by the Korbel Brothers of San Francisco. Its capacity output reached seventy thousand board feet of lumber per day. Also owned by the Korbel Brothers was the Arcata and Mad River Railroad, over which logs were hauled to the mill and finished lumber was hauled to their wharf on the bay.

The Milford Land and Lumber Company, incorporated in 1869, was located on Salmon Creek, a tributary of Humboldt Bay; a considerable portion of its timber was also owned by the company, which collected its cut logs in the shallows of the creek. When enough logs had been gathered, water was sluiced in, forcing the logs to move downstream to the mill. This mill's output reached approximately one million board feet per month.

The Eel River Valley Lumber Company's mill was located at Newburg, about two miles from Fortuna, in Humboldt County. The company owned four thousand acres of thick redwood forest in the Eel River Valley, and its output at the turn of the century reached fifty thousand board feet per day. The company also operated a shingle mill, capable of manufacturing sixty thousand shingles daily. The original mill was destroyed by fire, but a new mill, equipped with a band saw, proved a great success.

The Occidental Mill was situated in the city of Eureka, on Humboldt Bay. It was the oldest mill in Humboldt County. Its capacity was approximately fifty thousand feet of lumber a day. The company owned six miles of railroad line, over which logs were hauled and deposited in a small bay. From there the logs were rafted to the mill site. The company also owned three schooners—the *Occidental*, the *Fortuna*, and the *Ida McKay*. The *Occidental* and *Fortuna* hauled finished lumber to San Francisco.

Mills continued to spring up all over the region. The August 6, 1903, *San Francisco Call* announced, "Frederick Carney Jr. of Marinette, Wis., arrived here yesterday. Carney is a member of the H. Witbeck Lumber Company, which owns 6,700 acres on Grizzly Creek, this county. Negotiations are now under way for an extension of a branch of the Northwestern to reach the timber. When the arrangements are completed it is said mills will be built at once. The tract is one of the finest in the Redwood Belt and experts say it will cut 100,000 feet to the acre straight through."

In addition to the fact that new technology had to be employed in order to process redwood logs, just the act of "getting the logs out" in those early days was a monumental task. While the first fallers looked to smaller redwood trees to cut, as demand increased, they turned to larger and larger trees. According to the 1897 report released by the Redwood Lumber Manufacturers Association, the steps involved in taking down a redwood were painstakingly methodical, though quite dangerous.

The first cut was made by the axe, and this undercut determined the general direction the enormous tree would fall; this was particularly important when the tree stood close to other trees or stumps, as redwoods are prone to shatter if they don't hit the bed in the right way. As the trees' diameters increased, so did the size of axe handles; some hickory handles were as long as forty-two inches—ten inches longer than the length of a standard handle. Along with the increase in length, the axe heads became heavier, too. Some weighed as much as four pounds.

The cut was made several feet above ground, especially if the bottom swell of the tree was significantly larger than the general diameter of the tree. Sometimes scaffolding was built or springboards (boards jammed into a cut into the trunk) inserted around the base of the tree, upon which men could stand and continue the cut.

After the initial cut, two men with a huge crosscut saw felled the tree. Good teams could cut through a redwood as fast as one foot per hour. Wedges were driven in behind the saw as they worked the saw back and forth, hopefully insuring the direction of the immense tree's final and thunderous fall. The goal: to drop the tree without shattering it.

As one reporter who witnessed the fall of a redwood wrote, "The fall of a great redwood is startlingly like a prolonged thunder-crash, and is really a terrible sound."

Once laid to the ground, however, a whole army of workmen appeared to prepare the log for transportation. This was when the hard work of cutting up a redwood began.

The first workers were "ringers" who cut circles through the bark of the tree at intervals; next came the "peelers" who pried and stripped off the thick layer of bark (often a foot thick) with heavy steel bars. The next step was perhaps the most tedious and difficult. Because of their size and massive length, sawyers had to "buck" the felled redwoods into manageable lengths.

Ernest Ingersoll described this process in an article in the January 1883 *Harper's*:

> *The tree having been felled, men proceeded to trim away its top, and to split off its thick coat of bark. This can often be pried away almost without breaking it, except on top, so that a great cast, as it were, of the trunk is left in the bark, which lies there, after the logs are removed, like a huge ruined canoe. . . . The stripping of top branches and bark having been effected, the trunk is sawed into logs fifteen or*

It took a sizable crew to not only fell a redwood, but then to cut it into lengths and move it onto railroad cars.

twenty feet in length. A path is now cleared to them from the nearest road sufficiently good to take in six or eight yoke of oxen. This does not require to be a very good path either—though in some cases much labor and rough engineering is required for these wood roads—since the agility of the little oxen is quite wonderful when one notes what barriers of fallen trunks and what almost vertical slopes of hillside are surmounted.

Ingersoll continued, "Near the lower end of the log an iron hook called a 'dog' is driven in, where the drag-chain is attached. Then under a shower of such 'good mouth-filling oaths' as would have satisfied Falstaff, under resounding thwacks and proddings of an iron-tipped goad, the slipping and stumbling cattle snake the log endwise down the hill."

Generally, it is not just one log that is dragged: "Having arranged them in line at the head of the little gully which previous draggings have smoothed out, he chains together two, three, even five or six logs, and starts up the slow-moving cattle with a train behind them four or five rods long. . . . Ahead, he [the driver] swears at the meek Chinaman who travels ahead diligently wetting the ground to make it slippery."

Although technology improved with time, and chain saws were invented as early as 1905, two-handled saws remained the primary tools for felling and bucking redwoods until after World War II.

Since logging companies were paid by the number of logs successfully hauled to the mill sites, they tried to minimize waste; however, there was considerable waste left behind in the forests in these early years. Stumps, shattered trunks, or twisted, unrecoverable trees, along with the remnants from limbs and bark later burned as slash, probably equaled as much as 35 percent of the potential yield. In contrast, today's contractors are highly efficient and are able to salvage almost every part of their timber harvest.

Until railroads were built to haul logs, typically mills depended on water to move the logs to mill sites. Cut during the summer, the logs were stacked in nearby creeks, rivers, and/or reservoirs to await the winter rains or heavy flows. Sometimes the rivers were loaded with logs from bank to bank, but when the heavy rain finally came, the logs moved in one large

Before railroads could haul logs to mills, they were stored in reservoirs or moved by water (i.e. rivers).

mass down to the valleys or gulches below, powered by the rushing water. If there was an insufficient amount of water, "splash" dams might be built to store water, and when their gates were opened, the sudden release took the logs downstream.

As railroads began to link the northernmost reaches of California to San Francisco, they impacted the redwood timber industry significantly. By 1914 the Northwestern Pacific Railroad had finally connected Eureka and San Francisco. As a result, the cost of shipping milled lumber dropped, and that spurred the rate of cutting and logging of the redwoods. Everyone was interested in reaping the gold out of the redwood boom.

Within the forests, however, especially at higher elevations, the logs still had to be hauled or "snaked" down to the loading sites over well-constructed and well-maintained logging roads. This was especially true for redwood logging. With their mammoth size and weight, it was important to construct roads smooth and reliable enough to manage the heavy loads of redwood logs.

In the beginning "bulls," or teams of oxen, were used to drag a "train" of logs down these roads to where they would be loaded or lifted into waiting cars. Once the logs were maneuvered into position, they were pointed downhill and connected one to another with chains. Typically a six- or twelve-bull team would pull the load.

Wheeled vehicles were never used because of the rough terrain; instead, the logs had to be "yarded" along on skids or cross beams laid down to prevent the logs from digging into the earth. Sometimes oil or water was used, depending on conditions, to help lubricate the logs and keep them from building up friction. A "water packer" ran alongside the log train who poured water under the logs to keep them moving.

That this work was incredibly dangerous is no exaggeration. As retold in *The Home of the Redwood: A Souvenir of the Lumber Industry of California*, first printed in 1897:

> *It is a grand sight, twenty huge oxen tearing downhill, while just behind them come ten to fifteen great logs thundering after. It is a run for life or death . . . Should the leaders lag it means death to those behind; should an animal stumble and fall it may be the cause of killing half the team. Away they go, and for a few moments it seems a question whether team or train will reach the level ground first; but the road is well built and the driver has his team well in hand, and now at the bottom of the steep pitch they gradually "slow up," [and] lean against their yokes, and so they go, until the logs are safely landed*

Logs had to be hauled with great teams of oxen, as the terrain was too rough for wheeled vehicles.

at the railroad or the river. . . . The loads sometimes hauled by these ox teams are enormous. A train of seven logs hauled in Humboldt county in 1878 by A. A. Marks, teamster, scaled collectively 22,500 feet, board measure, of merchantable timber."

Though steam power was introduced as early as 1840, in the form of small steam-powered sawmills, steam locomotives didn't arrive until the 1870s, and a steam-powered winch system wasn't invented until 1881. The winch, however, revolutionized the redwood industry, especially after John Dolbeer introduced his "logging engine," also known as a "steam donkey." In time, Dolbeer's donkey was able to snake logs out of the forest, load them onto flatcars, and move them through the woods in a fraction of the time required for bull teams.

Later improvements brought about large stationary "bull donkeys," which could actually reel in logs from more than a mile away. The invention led to a more efficient system of yarding in logs, and even to replacing the bull teams. Eventually the invention led to the development of a system of cabling or connecting the donkey's cable to stumps or tall trees;

A steam donkey in Humboldt County helps snake logs onto a loading platform, circa 1910.

large logs were then skidded along the ground, while smaller logs were attached to aerial cables and pulled along through the air. Both of these techniques, however, required that all intervening trees were cleared out, thus "clear-cutting" became a routine practice.

The introduction of diesel-powered Caterpillar tractors, or "Cats," became the next revolutionary improvement in efficiency. Beginning in the late 1920s, these Cats were able to snake across ground quickly and remarkably. With a blade that was used to bulldoze roads or prepare log landings, a single Cat replaced as many as an eight-man crew.

Left behind, the mammoth stumps from the original old growth logging are a testimony to the size redwoods can achieve. While many an old stump is merely a shell of the tree it once was, some of these old growth stumps actually become the breeding ground for second-growth trees. Today there are people who are milling these giant stumps. According to G. F. Beranek in *High Climbers and Timber Fallers*, "When you take on one [old growth stump] you never know what you're going to run into. There's railroad spikes, old logging cable, chain, horseshoes, bottle and rocks."

Staking a Claim:
Ranching and Farming,
Then and Now

Good farmers, who take seriously their duties as stewards of Creation and of their land's inheritors, contribute to the welfare of society in more ways than society usually acknowledges, or even knows. These farmers produce valuable goods, of course; but they also conserve soil, they conserve water, they conserve wildlife, they conserve open space, they conserve scenery.

—WENDELL BERRY, *BRINGING IT TO THE TABLE:*
WRITINGS ON FARMING AND FOOD

LITTLE-KNOWN CALIFORNIA FACT: ALL THE GOLD PRODUCED IN THE century between 1840 and 1940 was worth less than the value of one year's agricultural output of the state in the 1960s.

Although timber and even fishing have been well-known industries of the northern California coastal areas, less understood by most people is the role that farming and ranching have played in and around the Redwood Belt. The attraction for many early immigrants was not the gold or lumber, or even the fishing. With the relatively mild climate, many settlers came with the desire to take up farming or ranching, in particular, dairy or livestock farming. Grains, fruits, and vegetables were also successful early crops.

Livestock became a mainstay in Humboldt and Del Norte Counties. Sheep and cattle did particularly well along the hilly coastal country and also east of the Redwood Belt. As with the miners, packers, and other whites, the early period of settlement was also laced with violence as ranchers and farmers overtook land that had been inhabited by the various tribes for generations. Many farmers and ranchers made their homes in areas now located within the Redwood National and State Parks or nearby valleys, surrounded by the backdrop of the majestic redwoods.

One such pioneer ranching family that established itself in the sheep business was the Lyons family. Jonathan Lyons, who first came to the northern California goldfields in the 1850s, settled in Hupa for a time, where he acquired a ranch and married Amelia Misket, a Hupa woman. The pair eventually moved to an old homestead on Redwood Creek, where Jonathan tried horse ranching. Finding himself losing more than he could earn back, he tried cattle ranching—again, to no avail. He moved down the canyon and up to the Bald Hills, where he tried raising sheep. With wool prices on the rise, Jonathan did well.

The Lyonses' adventure was just beginning. The family grew as the pair raised four sons. The ranch grew, too, and soon each of the sons was raising sheep as well. At one point, Jonathan's wool won a gold medal at the 1901 World's Exposition in Paris, France! Buyers came from all over to purchase their sheep.

Although the Lyonses' ranching operations were successful, the family endured their share of misfortune: The "Home Place" burned down three times, and bears and other predators frequently killed their sheep. Still, the ranch remained in the family for two more generations until the last of the Lyonses sold off the Home Place in 1972. This was after Austin Eugene, Jonathon's grandson, passed away.

Today, the hundred-year-old Lyons ranch is part of Redwood National Park, and although none of the family homes are standing, several old barns and shepherds' cabins remain as landmarks of the past.

Another historic family was the Tomlinson family. For forty-plus years, they also ran sheep on the rolling prairie. The large ranch house was built in 1919 and still stands. It's been told that the family's ten-foot-long cook stove could cook twenty-five hotcakes at one time; it also served to boil water used in boiling sheets on laundry day. The site was used as both a family home and stage stop. Freight wagons on their way to Orleans often stopped overnight.

As immigration swelled in the late nineteenth and early twentieth century, many Swiss-Italian immigrants came to work on farms across the bottomlands of the Mad and Eel Rivers, in the Orick valley, or along coastal areas. Even today many residents of the Ferndale (also known for a time as the "Cream City" for its dairies) area trace their ancestry to

Italian and Portuguese immigrants were among those who came and settled in many areas of coastal California.

these immigrants. The Portuguese also came to Humboldt County from the Azores; many found work on dairy ranches, while others took up jobs in the timber or fishing industry.

Small cattle ranches were established, too, and many continue today as multigenerational operations. A number of these operations also combined ranching and logging.

Jim Timmons, again from Andy Westfall's book *Humboldt Heartland*: "There was an opportunity for the sheep business and my dad had bought a band of sheep from Will Russ in the early 1920s and we enlarged that for a number of years until we had around 800 ewes on the ranch. We still have sheep that came from that original set of Dorsets."

After graduating with a degree in forestry from the University of California at Berkeley, Jim returned to the ranch. He continued:

We've been fortunate to have timber on this property. . . . Back in the early days, what I know of the 1920s—even 1930s—there was some recognition that these trees were gonna grow back again. One of the things people considered to be important was that the timber would come back faster if they had livestock on there for a while. That was borne out by the fact that when they finished logging in an area, they'd burn it, and try to clean off all that vegetation from the timber harvesting and then they'd sow it with grass seed and then they'd turn it over to the ranch. It kept the brush from growin' and the trees would seed into those grass prairies a whole lot better than they do with brush type competition. They had good results as far as the grass coming in and with stands of that on the ground the brush competition with timber was far less. A lot of that land seemed to be, if I remember the numbers, at least 15 years ahead as far as the timber comin' back in. We'd usually be able to graze a logged over area for 15 or 20 years.

Today there are few sheep ranches left. Changing economies, increased numbers of predators (in particular, coyote), and competing industries have all played a role in the decline of livestock and agricultural production. Still, many farmers and ranchers have continued to work the land.

Marlan Stover in *Humboldt Heartland* was born in 1920 and raised on his family's three-generation sheep ranch on Redwood Creek. After returning home to the ranch in 1967, Marlan and his father wintered around 1,800 sheep while his grandfather's uncle, when he arrived in 1872, was able to winter about 3,300 sheep.

Albert Hunt was born in 1927 on the family ranch, the Baker Creek Ranch. His story is also found in *Humboldt Heartland*, and he wrote about the work it took to keep the ranch going:

> *We cut all our own hay right there on the place. Dad'd plant maybe oats or wheat in the fall then it just depended on the rain to bring it on. If it was oats, he'd go check to see where the milk was in the seed. Ya just squeezed the seed head. If it hasn't got any milk in it, it isn't ready yet. Ya gotta catch it just right. . . . Then we'd start mowin'. . . . I remember drivin' a team in 1940. I think that was the first year mowin' hay, rakin' hay. Heck, it took four teams to do all the mowin' and rakin'—about 500 acres between the Dinsmore place and Sunny Basin. . . . We put it up all loose. We had to shock all the hay. We'd rake it into windrows with a dump rake and did all the shocking by hand with pitchforks. You just took a fork and you just turned that windrow over and made a pile here and then you just*

Pitching hay onto a wagon drawn by a two-horse team is a slow process.

piled more hay on top until you had a stack about three foot wide and three foot high.

In parts of Humboldt County, dairy farming reigned. Many of the farmers drained marshlands or cleared valley bottoms. In the twentieth century, dairy cooperatives took over much of the processing operations, and dairy products such as cheese, butter, and powdered milk became important area exports.

Humboldt Creamery, for example, was founded in 1929 by Peter Philipsen. It was established as a local association of 152 separate dairy farms, and even up until 2009, the creamery's production was based on 50 relatively small family dairies in both Humboldt and Del Norte Counties. The co-op provided fresh milk for local markets, then moved to producing butter and powdered milk for export. Unique to this region was the ability to pasture cows nine months of the year versus having to supplement feed and grain in areas where the climate is less mild.

In 2004 Humboldt Creamery was producing more than ten million gallons of ice cream in addition to milk, butter, and cheese, and by 2008 it began marketing nationally, but financial and legal issues in 2009 affected the creamery's production. In order to survive, some assets of the company were sold off, but the original site in Ferndale continues to flourish.

From its earliest days of settlement, Humboldt County was also known for its variety and quality of fruit. Pears, plums, peaches, and berries did well, but apples were an extremely successful crop and a major export. In the early days, apples traveled by barge from Mattole Valley down the Eel River to be shipped to San Francisco.

Conservation Grows Out of Fear

Hail, Monarch of the Woods!
A thousand years
Have sped since first you reached forth to the sky,
And still your trunk its giant frame uprears,
As though it mocked at time and would not die.
Your roots defy the earthquake's shock, your crest
Denies the puissance of the winter blast;
Year after year your lordly branches dressed
Their phalanxes in green, and still you cast
A mighty shadow 'thwart the tangled glen.
Rooted in majesty for aye you'd stand.
But now your doom is told—lo! pygmy men
Will mar your kingly state with ruthless hand;
The widowed hills and woods will mourn their chief,
And tears distil from every blade and leaf.
      —DR. C. W. DOYLE, "THE REDWOOD," AUGUST 25, 1894

AS LOGGING BECAME MORE AND MORE EFFICIENT, LEAVING BEHIND A graveyard of old stumps and clear-cut areas, many people became alarmed. Would there be no redwoods left? Would these massive sentinels survive the onslaught of greed and technology?

Stewart Udall underlined the tragic fall of the redwood empire when he wrote in the foreword to *The Last Redwoods*, published in 1963: "We are a nation of woodsmen who made Paul Bunyan a national folklore hero."

And, though efforts to preserve these trees actually began even before the industrialized timber industry took hold, a national redwoods park was not established for years.

Many early proponents tried, however, to bring awareness to the beauty and character of these giants—including the giant sequoia. An oft-overlooked effort to protect the redwoods was initiated by Joseph Welch in 1867, when he purchased a site near the present-day town of Felton, in the Santa Cruz Mountains, which had first been visited by John C. Frémont in February 1846. According to one record, Frémont spent the night in a burned-out hollow redwood, then carved an *F* in its bark to mark the spot.

When Frémont ran for president in 1856, the fame of the Felton, California, redwood grew as well. Welch purchased the property and developed it as a tourist attraction, complete with cabins, dining hall, and pavilion. Later, when the Southern Pacific Railroad was built in 1880, it passed through Welch's property. Passengers could almost reach out and touch the giant trees as the train whirred through the stands of redwoods.

Perhaps the most famous of all early conservationists was John Muir. Although his work related more to preservation of the giant sequoias than to the coast redwoods, no doubt his writings helped capture the general public's attention and influenced conservationists who followed after him.

Indeed, he once declared that only Uncle Sam could save the giant trees.

Others who brought light to the issue of saving California's redwoods was Redwood City newspaper editor Ralph S. Smith, who, circa 1886, proposed establishing a twenty-thousand-acre California state park near Santa Cruz, not only to satisfy tourists, but also to be used for scientific study. Critics maintained that Smith's zeal in establishing a forest reserve was stimulated by the Spring Valley Water Company's desire to secure a permanent cover for their Pescadero watershed; but whatever his motivation, Smith was clearly one of the first vocal proponents of a state park and was willing to put in print the idea of saving a share of the redwoods for future generations.

Smith wrote for his own paper, the *Redwood City Times and Gazette*, as well as for the *San Francisco Chronicle*:

> *Among the most beautiful of all coniferous trees is the redwood of California, the* Sequoia sempervirens, *as the botanists call it. It is purely indigenous, and with the mammoth Sequoias form the distinctive feature of the forests of this State. For many years it has been*

The Legacy of John Muir

John Muir emigrated with his family from Scotland at age eleven to live on a farm in Wisconsin. Although his conservation focus was directed toward preserving multiple wilderness sites throughout the West and Pacific Northwest, his writings and concern for the preservation of redwoods made him a strong voice for preserving vast stands of old growth redwoods.

He wrote, regarding the Pacific Northwest Alaska, that a portion of wilderness ought to "be set apart and protected for public use forever, containing at least a few hundreds of these noble pines, spruces, and firs. Happy will be the men, who, having the power and the love and the benevolent forecast to do this, will do it. They will not be forgotten. The trees and their lovers will sing their praises, and generations yet unborn will rise up and call them blessed."

In this regard, Muir is most famous: He envisioned a system of national parks and forests that would conserve the wonders of the American wilderness.

According to the National Park Service website:

Muir popularized a radically new concept of American land use and conservation. His writings moved presidents, congressmen, and ordinary Americans to action. President Cleveland drew on Muir's work to establish thirteen forest reserves and what became the US Forest Service. Muir was directly involved in establishing Yosemite [1890], Sequoia

the chief source of the lumber supply of the State, and in consequence the redwood forests have been enormously depleted. It is known to comparatively few that within fifty miles of this city, in a southerly direction, there is a redwood forest of one hundred and eighty square miles, or over one hundred and twenty thousand acres. The northern two thirds of this tract is almost virgin, there having been but slight inroads made upon it. This tract begins on Pescadero Creek, forty-six miles from San Francisco. Its western edge reaches to within about four miles of the Pacific Ocean, on an average, and it crosses the sum-

[1890], Mount Rainier [1899], and Grand Canyon [1908] National Parks. Muir is often called the "Father of Our National Park System."

In 1892, he helped found, together with Robert Underwood Johnson, the Sierra Club, to protect the newly created Yosemite National Park and to "do something for wildness and make the mountains glad." Muir and the Sierra Club fought many battles to protect Yosemite and the Sierra Nevada. He served as the Club's president until his death in 1914.

Muir personally knew three presidents and many writers and philosophers. He exerted his greatest influence on Theodore Roosevelt. In 1901, Muir published *Our National Parks*, a book that brought him to President Theodore Roosevelt's attention. In 1903, Roosevelt visited Muir in Yosemite. Together, they laid the foundation of Roosevelt's innovative conservation programs. Soon after that meeting, Roosevelt started on a course of action that established 148 million acres of national forest, 5 national parks and 23 national monuments during his presidency.

When Muir began his conservation career in the late 1880s, America saw its wild lands as reservoirs of commodities needed to drive its industrial engines. When he died in 1914, the Nation was committed in spirit, to the wise use of its natural resources. Today Muir's influence lives on in the public's appreciation and support of America's wild places.

mits and covers the slopes of the Coast Range lying between the bay and the ocean.

Smith also wrote that he would "undertake, if the State will appropriate a reasonably generous sum for the purchase of this [proposed] tract, to be placed at the disposal of the Forestry Commission, to raise an equal amount by subscription for the same purpose."

Two Californians who supported Smith's call for a park included former governor and Stanford University's founder, Leland Stanford, and Joaquin Miller, a poet and naturalist who pushed for conservation all over northern California. Sadly, the state legislature adjourned their session that year without taking any action. As a result, much of central California's redwood region fell to more and more loggers.

In 1885 California established a Board of Forestry in order to help curb wasteful logging; in 1899 Gifford Pinchot, of Pennsylvania, long considered the "father" of national forests, began conducting studies under the US Department of Agriculture. Pinchot later pushed President Theodore Roosevelt to demand the preservation of the Monterey Forest Reserve in 1906.

In 1900, commissioned by a London magazine to take photographs of the Santa Cruz redwoods, Andrew P. Hill, of San Jose, traveled to the Fremont Big Tree Grove. Hill was a well-known artist throughout California and had long admired the redwoods; as early as 1877 he had painted the group of trees that stood near the Hotel de Redwood in the Santa Cruz Mountains.

Unfortunately the owners of the property refused to let him photograph the trees. Having seen the redwoods and resenting the owners' refusal to allow him access, he decided that the trees, being natural wonders, ought to belong to the people of the state. On a train later that day, he wrote to journalist Josephine Clifford McCracken, a letter she then published in the *Santa Cruz Sentinel* along with an article urging people to rally around the cause. Hill also wrote to the Santa Cruz Board of Trade, imploring them to "pass a resolution recommending that Congress be petitioned to make the purchase of the Fremont Grove."

The secretary of the Board of Trade responded to Hill's plea, adding that, "As your enthusiasm is for the smaller proposition, so in ratio will it increase for the larger." Encouraged, Hill then wrote to the *San Jose Mercury*, calling for a meeting of interested parties. The meeting was held at the Stanford University Library, with university president David Starr Jordan, scientists, and other influential people in attendance. A surveying committee was appointed, headed by Hill and Carrie Stevens Walter from the San Jose Woman's Club. Hill also learned that a pair of university professors had examined the Big Basin trees and mapped the area, and were likewise calling for their preservation.

As Carrie Stevens Walter wrote, "Once gone, no human power or ingenuity can replace them. Even the most callous-minded materialist does not love to think of this swirling globe as a treeless place."

The *Mountain Echo* of May 26, 1900, later reported:

> *The visiting party in the Big Basin last week held an enthusiastic meeting the night before breaking camp and formed an organization to be known as the Sempervirens Club. The object of the club is to work for the preservation of the Big Basin and adjacent region as a public park. Thus was the Sempervirens Club of California organized at the foot of Slippery Rock, just across the stream now called Sempervirens Creek, and the place was named Sempervirens Camp. The zeal and enthusiasm of this club knew no bounds, and it compelled the attention of the State.*

In a few months the Sempervirens Club had attained a large membership. The club, even today, is California's oldest land trust. Clearly, as a result of its persistent outreach to the public and politicians alike, the California Redwood Park (aka Reserve)—later named Big Basin Redwoods State Park in 1927—was established in 1902. For the first time the state acquired 3,800 acres of ancient redwood forests.

Moreover, in March of 1905, an act to create a new State Board of Forestry and to provide for the protection and management of public and private forestlands within the State of California was passed. The first State Board of Forestry had been created in 1885 but abolished in 1893.

According to Betts and Foster, coauthors of the *History of the CDF Archaeology Program 1970-2004*, "This legislation established a new Board of Forestry, created the position of State Forester, and placed Big Basin State Park under the authority of the Board. The State Forester was empowered to fight fires, plant trees, care for the state parks, hire assistants, and appoint citizens as fire wardens."

One of the provisions of the act also stated that, "if the government of the United States or any individual or corporation shall, at any time, donate or entrust to the State of California, for state park or state forest reserve purposes, any tract or tracts of wholly or partially wooded land, such tract or tracts of land shall be administered at the expense of the state, as provided by law."

Although the original twenty-thousand-acre state park that Ralph S. Smith proposed did not materialize, the bill that created the California Redwood Park was passed. The 1901 bill also established the California Redwood Park Commission, which purchased and received (through donations) an additional 3,901 acres from the Big Basin Lumber Company in 1906. In 1916 another 3,785 acres were taken from federal control and added to Big Basin Redwoods State Park.

The Sempervirens Club continued to work to protect redwood forestlands adjacent to Big Basin, hoping to establish a much "greater park" that expanded the boundaries of Big Basin Redwoods State Park. They hoped to purchase privately owned parcels and extend the park westward to the coast. In the words of Andrew P. Hill, Big Basin would become "one great playground for the people of California and the world."

As noted in 1912 by Arthur A. Taylor, secretary of the California Redwood Park Commission, regarding the establishment of the California Redwood Park (aka Big Basin Redwoods State Park):

A too common idea of a forest is of sombrous silence. There is silence in this place, but it is a silence in which the voices of creation can be heard. There is majesty and sublimity in these time-defying trees, but as we have tried to show, there is also in this wood beauty and color, and woodland life in many manifestations. This forest is an aggregation of arboreal wonders. It is moreover a cathedral, a university, a sanatorium, a source of solace to the soul, an inspiration to the intellect, a tonic to the body.

Clearly, the initiative it took to establish Big Basin Redwoods State Park inspired others in California to take up the call for increased redwood preservation north of San Francisco.

In 1911 John E. Raker, a California Democratic representative to the US Congress, became the first politician on a federal level to introduce the concept of a national redwood park. A former district attorney and superior court judge, he served seven terms in Congress until his death in 1926.

William Kent was a political reformer and conservationist. Born in 1864, Kent was raised near the base of Mount Tamalpais, north of San Francisco. Though he went on to become an important politician in Chicago, he eventually returned to California to settle permanently. In 1903 he learned that a section of virgin timber in a nearby narrow canyon was about to be logged. Determined to save the trees, he borrowed $45,000 and bought the property. When he heard that a water company might dam a creek below the property, Kent decided to donate the land to the federal government.

The federal government was not sure how to accept the land or how to administer it, so Kent appealed to both John Muir and Theodore Roosevelt. However, there was no money for improvements or administration, and Kent stepped in and paid the cost of a road to access the property. His one demand was that the monument be named in honor of John Muir.

A reception was held in Kent's honor, as recorded by the *San Francisco Call*, November 23, 1908:

> *William Kent, who gave Redwood Canyon, now known as Muir Woods, to the federal government, was the guest of honor last night at a reception given in San Rafael by the Native Sons of the Golden West, who have taken a deep interest in the preservation of the natural wonders of the state and who honored Kent for his generosity in turning over to the people the majestic stand of redwoods near Mill Valley. . . . Joaquin Miller read a poem for the occasion. . . . And then lantern slides depicting scenes in the canyon were displayed.*

In a letter to Kent in 1908, President Roosevelt wrote:

> *My Dear Mr. Kent: I have just received from Secretary Garfield your very generous letter enclosing the gift of Redwood Canyon to the National Government to be kept as a perpetual park for the preservation of the giant redwoods therein and to be named the Muir National*

Monument. You have doubtless seen my proclamation of January 9th, instant, creating this monument. I thank you most heartily for this singularly generous and public-spirited action on your part. All Americans who prize the natural beauties of the country and wish to see them preserved undamaged, and especially those who realize the literally unique value of the groves of giant trees, must feel that you have conferred a great and lasting benefit upon the whole country.

Using the Antiquities Act, which gives the executive branch the power to establish national monuments, President Roosevelt was able to accept Kent's gift of 295 acres of redwoods sheltered in Redwood Canyon at the base of Mount Tamalpais, saving it from the flood waters that might have come had the water company successfully dammed the creek. Today, the monument has been expanded to include an additional section of land—also given by Kent—making Muir Woods, located about an hour north of San Francisco, the most visited redwood grove in California.

Subsequently, Kent was elected to the US Congress. One of his most important endeavors in Congress was to help author the bill that established the National Park Service in 1916. After leaving Congress, he

The Antiquities Act

The Antiquities Act of 1906 was the first law to acknowledge the importance of archeological sites in America. The act was passed out of deep concern for the mishandling and loss or looting of artifacts and locations that had (and have) great historical and cultural value. The movement to establish such a law began during the last decades of the nineteenth century when archaeologists and other scientists and educators became alarmed at the careless and irresponsible destruction of various sites throughout the country, but in particular, the Southwest and the West.

The act gave the president of the United States the power to identify and designate those locations particularly sensitive and fragile—sites that, if lost, could not be redeemed. It also obligated helped found the Save-the-Redwoods League in 1918. He also ran for the Senate, but was defeated. However, his efforts to preserve the redwoods continued; after donating the land that became the famed Muir Woods, he pushed for the creation of a state park to adjoin the Muir Woods.

Of course, there were many more obstacles to face and overcome in the continued quest to save both the sequoia and the coast redwoods. Sadly, California Redwood Park, which was being supervised by the newly established Redwood Park Commission, burned in 1904—a wildfire that consumed 1,200 acres in one month. As a result, the new California governor chose to abolish the commission and turn control of the park over to the State Board of Forestry, but the board was soon accused of logging off not only dead or dying redwoods, but live trees as well.

According to a history compiled by C. Raymond Clar titled "California Government and Forestry" in 1959, "It is somewhat doubtful . . . if any Board of Forestry was greatly enthusiastic about engaging in the difficult and specialized business of supervising and maintaining land for purely recreational purposes. . . . Concurrently, with the work of acquiring and managing parks, the Board of Forestry was decidedly interested in the acquisition of State Forests. Chairman Pardee was explicit in November of 1920 as to the firm intention of the Board of Forestry to

the federal government to protect those sites, including landmarks, structures, and objects of historic value, by designating them "National Monuments."

President Theodore Roosevelt, a conservationist himself, signed the Antiquities Act into law on June 8, 1906. As the first such effort to protect natural resources in the United States, it established the legal precedence for managing and caring for sites, collections, and other resources across the nation.

The act is still in effect and has been used at different points in the country's history. According to the National Park Service website, "Today, many different organizations cooperate in diverse partnerships, including governments at the Federal, state, tribal and local levels; professional and scholarly groups; and communities. In shaping public policy to protect a broad array of cultural and natural resources, the impact of the Antiquities Act is unmatched."

"Bird Man"

Up until 1918, not one single redwood tree had been protected by the state in either northern Humboldt or Del Norte counties. Logging was king, and any preservation attempt up to that time had not been successful. With the creation of the Save-the-Redwoods League in 1918, however, along with the changing attitudes of the California public, a new era was dawning.

In Humboldt County, one very concerned conservationist was Charles "Bird Man" Kellogg, who initiated his own campaign to save the redwoods. Disturbed by the amount of logging going on around him, Kellogg—an entertainer who was known for his unusual "birdlike" voice and vaudeville acts—decided that "since all the world could not come to the forest, I kept thinking and thinking through many years how to take the forests out into the world."

request $150,000 at repeated sessions of the Legislature for the purchase of cut-over lands."

In its estimation the Board would then have jurisdiction over the management and protection of timberlands, ensuring a continuous timber supply. Lumbermen supported the Board in its requests to the State.

In 1923, another report on the status of forestry was submitted. In it, the new state forester wrote, "The former Board [of Forestry] recommended that $150,000 be appropriated for the purpose of acquiring cutover lands for State Forests, but this recommendation was not followed up, due to the popular demand for the acquisition of virgin redwood timber for park purposes."

In 1927 the California Redwoods Park became part of the newly created State Park System, and the park was renamed Big Basin Redwoods State Park. Also in 1927, one year before William Kent died, California established Mount Tamalpais State Park, to which Kent again donated land.

In his honor, a tree in Muir Woods was dubbed the "Kent Tree," although it was not a redwood but a Douglas fir. The tree had been Kent's favorite, and at its base sits a plaque that reads: "William Kent: who

In 1917, with the support of *Sunset* magazine, Kellogg began touring in a motor home fashioned from a single redwood tree. The superintendent of Pacific Lumber even assisted Kellogg in the selection of his redwood, a fallen tree located on its Bull Creek Flats property on the Eel River. It took Kellogg several weeks to trim a log 360 feet long and 11 feet in diameter into a 22-foot section, hollowed out and chiseled into a finished "motor home." The "Travel Log" was loaded onto a truck donated by Nash Motors. The home boasted windows, beds, even a kitchenette and a small bathroom.

Over a two-year period, from 1917 through 1918, Kellogg toured the entire East Coast. He also sold World War I bonds as he touted his message of redwood conservation and performed for audiences. The motor home was stored for seventy-five years after Kellogg's retirement; recently the Humboldt Redwoods Interpretive Association restored the unique Travel Log, and it is now on display at Humboldt Redwoods State Park.

gave these woods and other natural beauty sites to perpetuate them for people who love the out-of-doors."

To this day Kent is remembered for his contributions and efforts to preserve and establish Muir Woods and to help create the National Park Service.

Through these early and varied efforts, the notion of preserving the redwoods and/or establishing a national park was elevated. While the Sempervirens Club was the first broad-based civic effort to establish a redwood park in the Santa Cruz Mountains, followed by William Kent's gift of Muir Woods, it would be the Save-the-Redwoods League that initiated the greatest efforts to save the majestic coastal redwood groves of Humboldt and Del Norte Counties in northern California.

The year was 1917, and the Club was once again gathered under the redwoods for its annual retreat. The Bohemians were famous for their "Jinks," dramatic capers performed each year under the canopy of redwoods, as touted in an article that appeared in the *San Francisco Call* in August 1902: "Last night . . . the latest specimen of Bohemian genius was produced. . . . The drama expresses in allegory Bohemia's protection of the redwoods, and is titled 'The Man in the Forest,' but better known as the 'Indian Jinks.'"

Included in the group were four influential men: poet and conservationist Joaquin Miller; Henry Fairfield Osborn, president of the American Museum of Natural History in New York City; Dr. John C. Merriam, paleontologist at the University of California; and Madison Grant, chairman of the New York Zoological Society. Merriam and Grant were also members of the Boone and Crockett Club, which had been created by Theodore Roosevelt in 1889.

After leaving the retreat in Sonoma County, the four headed north, along the newly established Redwood Highway, to visit the mammoth

The Legacy of John C. Merriam

"As I stood once with a group of friends looking into a redwood forest, which we had come far to see, in swift panorama the history of these trees and of their surroundings as I knew them passed before me, stage after stage, from the remote past." —John C. Merriam, *The Living Past*

John C. Merriam was born in Iowa in 1869, the son of the local postmaster and proprietor of a general store. Ever fascinated by nature, as a young man he began collecting fossils. Later he graduated from Lenox College in Iowa, then went on to the University of California at Berkeley to study botany and geology.

In 1901 one of his lectures inspired Miss Annie Montague Alexander, who later helped Merriam finance his expeditions to Mount Shasta in 1902 and 1903 in addition to his 1905 expedition to Nevada, where he discovered twenty-five specimens of ichthyosaur, many of them still considered pristine.

In 1903 Merriam became a member of the Boone and Crockett Club, a conservation group established by Theodore Roosevelt and George Bird Grinnell, which carved the way for conservation of the redwoods through its active membership.

Obviously concerned about nature, Merriam also cofounded the Save-the-Redwoods League and served as its president from 1921 to 1944. In 1922 his concern over the future of Humboldt redwoods. The new Redwood Highway was both a curse and a blessing in their eyes: It not only made the redwoods more accessible and, therefore, more likely to be saved, but it also meant that a number of big trees now stood as obstacles to the highway's development. And it meant that more people would very likely want to settle in the region.

The trip along the Redwood Highway became a watershed event as the four men and the dream of saving the redwoods was born. After seeing firsthand the destruction left behind in the wake of logging the redwoods, the men wrote to California's governor, William D. Stephens, about the impressive nature of the trees and what was happening as a result of the logging practices of the day.

County was inspired by what he had witnessed in the way of redwood destruction around the San Francisco Bay area. He became determined to help preserve as much old growth and virgin stands of redwood as he could.

Merriam also spent twenty-six years as a professor at Berkeley, but was so drawn to nature that he wanted to see parks managed primarily for the education and inspiration of visitors. He wanted them to appreciate the continuity of life in the past to life in the present. According to Stephen R. Mark, in *Preserving the Living Past: John C. Merriam's Legacy in the State and National Parks*, "Even if some ancient plant and animal species had given way to those presently occupying the forest, he said, ancient redwood trees could render the geological time scale comprehensible to visitors who contemplated the past according to a human time scale."

Merriam helped spur the passage of the 1928 state bond measure that provided that the state match private donations to purchase selected stands of redwoods. The measure was a significant step forward for both the Save-the-Redwoods League and preservationists up and down the state, and helped to ignite the public.

Always concerned with reaching the visitor through education, and not accepting the notion that land could merely be preserved without purpose, Merriam effected many of the policies and procedures the National Park Service developed over time.

The Redwood Highway, officially dedicated in 1923, opened access to travelers even as it brought more recognition to the redwoods.
FRANK PATTERSON, PHOTOGRAPHER

Articles appeared in *National Geographic* magazine, describing the devastation left by loggers. Following that, Albert Atwood, Joseph Hergesheimer, and Samuel Blythe also began writing about the devastation of redwood forests for the *Saturday Evening Post*. The result: The American public was stirred, and there was a flood of two-dollar contributions to Save-the-Redwoods League. In addition, large donations came in from such men as Stephen Mather, the director of the National Park Service, as well as from William Kent, and John Phillips of Wenham, Massachusetts.

Determined to move forward, League representatives traveled to Washington, DC, and met with Secretary of the Interior Franklin K. Lane—who agreed to become the League's president. Other influential members of the League included Robert G. Sproul, president of the University of California at Berkeley, and William Kent.

With the nation's focus still on post–World War I concerns, Congress was not interested in pursuing the idea of a national redwood park, and because the US government had never purchased private lands for parks, the cause was not taken up on a federal level. Two proposals for a national park were defeated in the Senate.

One bill was introduced by Congressman Clarence F. Lea of Santa Rosa, California, who introduced House Resolution No. 159 in 1919. The redwood "resolution" was adopted in May 1920, but because no money was involved, the Senate was not required to approve the measure. The Secretary of the Interior, however, was instructed to investigate the possible locations for such a proposed national park. Likewise, the Secretary of Agriculture was instructed to conduct the investigation through the Forest Service. This was accomplished in what was called the "Reddington Report" at the end of 1920.

The three-man party selected to study the proposal included R. F. Hammett, assistant district forester for the US Forest Service in California (who soon resigned to become secretary of the Redwood Lumbermen's Association); M. B. Pratt, deputy state forester for California; and Donald Bruce, associate professor of Forestry at UC Berkeley. The cost of the study was underwritten by the Save-the-Redwoods League.

In 1920, the committee examined a number of locations in northern California, including areas along the Klamath River and the South Fork Eel River, as well as along Prairie Creek, Redwood Creek, and Big Lagoon. Their recommendation: a 64,000-acre national park on the Lower Klamath River. Part of the appeal lay in the government's control of Indian lands that would make acquisition less complicated. In addition, the location featured superior stands of redwoods and a scenic and navigable river.

The committee also recommended the establishment of a 1,800-acre "administrative unit" on the South Fork of the Eel River in order to protect the pristine groves along the proposed state highway.

On the other hand, sites along Prairie Creek and at Big Lagoon, while impressive, did not seem as desirable. And the Redwood Creek location was dismissed altogether.

Back in Washington, the report was met with some favorability; however, the Senate refused to spend public funds to purchase private property, especially "economically productive" lands.

Though Stephen Mather of the NPS and proponents of a national park were disappointed, the members of Save-the-Redwoods League were not content to sit passively until some future moment in time. In their minds, the situation was critical. More and more old growth redwoods were being felled and logged off. Merriam, Osborn, and others hoped the League could purchase prime redwood tracts, especially in Humboldt and Del Norte counties, and donate them as parks, especially since state law now allowed the government to match any charitable donations for parklands.

Immediately the League began calling upon timber companies to impose a voluntary logging moratorium in those groves located closest to the highway. In addition, Mather and William Kent announced that each would put up $15,000 for the purchase of stands of redwoods. Even Humboldt County followed suit soon after.

In 1920 the Save-the-Redwoods League was incorporated as a nonprofit corporation, and membership quickly reached four thousand. It managed to purchase four tracts of land, including: stands in the Mill Creek drainage near the Oregon border; a strip of old growth timber in Del Norte County; and in Prairie Creek where a herd of Roosevelt elk were known to live; plus along the South Fork Eel River with groves of massive trees.

More lands were purchased by Save-the-Redwoods League or were acquired through donations from wealthy groups and/or families and individuals—most dedicated to honor another person or group.

The League also hired a public relations specialist—Newton B. Drury—who led the public campaign to raise awareness of the plight of the redwoods, particularly the most impressive stands. In a little pamphlet he later published in 1945, titled "Saving the Redwoods," he would write regarding the creation of the League, "The Save-the-Redwoods League 'started from scratch.' When in 1917 John C. Merriam made his now historic trip with Madison Grant and Henry Fairfield Osborn by automobile over wagon roads that have since developed into the celebrated Redwood Highway, not one stick of timber in that region, comprising what many now consider the finest forest in the world, was publicly owned."

Newton B. Drury

Newton Bishop Drury was born on April 9, 1889, in San Francisco. He attended the University of California, Berkeley, and graduated in 1912. While overseas with the US Army Balloon Corps during World War I, he witnessed the terrible devastation of Europe's landscape. What he saw affected him deeply.

When Newton returned home after the war, he and his brother Aubrey went into business, and in 1919 established the Drury Brothers Company, an advertising and public relations agency. That same year the Drury brothers were asked to manage the newly established Save-the-Redwoods League.

Newton accepted the job as executive director, a position he would hold for twenty years. Enterprising and ambitious, Newton Drury is credited with helping the League to eventually obtain a $6 million bond measure that was passed by California voters allowing the League to purchase redwood property.

Drury, who had refused the job of director of the National Park Service in 1933, accepted the position in 1940, making him the fourth director since the NPS's creation, but the first without prior national park experience. During World War II he worked to protect the national parks' resources. He also opposed NPS involvement with areas he felt did not meet national park standards. Such differences of opinion led to Drury's resignation in 1951.

The Newton B. Drury Scenic Parkway is a nine-mile two-lane road through Prairie Creek Redwoods State Park, which is located fifty miles north of Eureka. Completed in 1993, it honors Drury and his efforts to help create Redwood National and State Parks. Mount Drury, in the Mount San Jacinto State Park in Riverside County, California, was also named for him.

At the same time, the Board of Forestry made an official note in its minutes of February 24, 1921, that several individuals were anxious to "donate redwood land in Humboldt County provided it would be administered as permanent recreation land by the Board of Forestry." At least the Board had acknowledged a vague interest in the creation of a redwood park system. Legislation was later introduced and Solon Williams pursued the project "vigorously." The bill was introduced in 1921, but languished, even as a Redwood Preservation Bill was introduced and then passed, submitted by F. J. Cummings, a dairyman from Ferndale.

Governor Stephens signed the Redwood Preservation Bill in 1921. Included in the bill was $300,000 for the purchase of land running adjacent to the newly developed Redwood Highway in both Humboldt and Mendocino counties. The money and the land would fall under the jurisdiction of the Board of Forestry, and the Board was authorized to "purchase land, by condemnation procedure if necessary. Gifts of timber-bearing land and other contributions from any source could be accepted by the Board for the purpose of establishing, maintaining, and supervising the redwood parks. The Board could [also] make rules and regulations necessary to meet the provisions of the act."

These early purchases protected groves that were otherwise going to be logged.

According to C. Raymond Clar, "For park enthusiasts this was the moment of 'Now or Never,' and that was their slogan. Fortunately for posterity these were a dedicated people who seemed to perform miracles in Sacramento largely because of their selfless enthusiasm and zeal in working for the future public welfare."

A report in *The Timberman* related the signing of Assembly Bill 80 on June 3, 1921: "During the last hours before the time elapsed for the signing of the bill, proponents of the measure gathered at the Capitol and the anxiety was at fever pitch because no word had come from the governor as to whether he would give his approval to the large appropriation. It was within two hours of the closing time when Mrs. Stephens, wife of the governor, called on the telephone from the state mansion to ask whether the measure had been signed. And almost immediately announcement was made that the governor had given the measure his approval."

After this landmark decision, according to Clar, "the Save-the-Redwoods League was a virtual arm of the Board of Forestry in persuading, negotiating, and investigating among landowners and potential donors. This cooperative venture seems to have worked with remarkable smoothness."

Board of Forestry minutes in 1921 acknowledged member Solon Williams with a note of thanks "for the efficient work he is doing in the acquisition of the redwood timber for the State in Humboldt and Mendocino counties."

Sadly, Williams, who retired in 1923, died in 1926. The Board wrote that his "untiring efforts and zealous devotion" had helped make acquisition of the northern redwood parks possible. In 1929, in his honor, a 265-acre grove, the Solon H. Williams Memorial Grove in Humboldt Redwood State Park, was dedicated.

In August 1921, Dr. John C. Phillips donated the funds needed for the purchase of a grove in memory of his brother-in-law, Colonel Reynaud C. Bolling, who had been killed in World War I. The Bolling Memorial Grove in Humboldt Redwoods State Park was dedicated on August 6, 1921.

In 1923, the newly appointed Board of Forestry members passed a "resolution of commendation" to the Save-the-Redwoods League for "its endeavor to secure additional redwood forests for park purposes."

There were a number of legislative attempts to push for more park and forestry acquisitions beginning in 1923; however, very little State money was appropriated. Purchases made in 1923 and 1924 were groves that would later become part of Prairie Creek Redwoods State Park (established 1923) and Del Norte Coast Redwoods State Park (established 1925) and were accomplished through negotiations with private landowners; however, until John D. Rockefeller Jr. stepped in to provide a $1 million donation, the Save-the-Redwoods League was unable to negotiate the purchase of the Dyerville and Bull Creek Flats, land that was owned by the Pacific Lumber Company.

In addition to Rockefeller's donation, Humboldt County's Board of Supervisors agreed to help. A court order prohibited further logging on the Flats, even though the actual purchase of the groves didn't occur until 1931.

But in 1931, Major Frederick Russell Burnham commissioned a survey of the redwoods near Bull Flat Creek. When a 364-foot redwood was located, the California State Park Commission dedicated the tree to the founders of the Save-the-Redwoods League on September 13,

Because of John D. Rockefeller's donation of $1 million, the Save-the-Redwoods League was able to negotiate the purchase of Bull Creek Flats.
FRANK PATTERSON, PHOTOGRAPHER

1931: "As a living monument symbolizing eternal life and duration of our gratitude."

In response, Burnham declared: "It is an ancient and racial urge that has brought us together today in the shade of this far Western forest like the druids of old." The Founders' Tree immediately became one of the most popular trees in the Redwood Belt. Its height measurement has since been revised to 346.1 feet.

In the end it took $1.8 million in State Park Bond funds and $1.4 million in private gifts—including Rockefeller's $1 million contribution—to purchase the 13,629 acres from Pacific Lumber. Even today, the Rockefeller Forest is the largest contiguous old growth redwood forest in the world.

Continued efforts to pass legislation continued to frustrate park enthusiasts and proponents. In 1927, however, Governor C. C. Young requested, and obtained, the creation of a Department of Natural Resources. Further action was passed, as well, which defined the purpose

The Founders' Tree measures 346.1 feet high and is
dedicated to the founders of the Save-the-Redwoods
League.

FRANK PATTERSON, PHOTOGRAPHER

of a State Park "system." It stated that "all authority to acquire land for
parks and to manage park land was herewith vested in the State Park
Commission working through the Department of Natural Resources."

In addition, a new survey was ordered, requiring the Director of Natural Resources, through the Park Commission, "to make a survey of all

lands suitable for parks 'for the ultimate development of a comprehensive, well-balanced state park system.'"

Finally, in 1927, a law providing for the issuance and sale of $6 million in State bonds to finance the purchase of forestlands was passed. In addition, the $6 million bond that passed overwhelmingly by voters in 1928 mandated that every dollar collected from private donations be matched by the State.

The Save-the-Redwood League supported both the efforts to establish a statewide park system and the passage of the bond issue. The California Redwood Association and the National Lumber Manufacturers Association likewise joined forces with the League, which is a testament to the kinds of relationships that the League had managed to establish with various companies and individuals in the lumber industry.

The League had, in fact, made it clear that it was not trying to save every redwood or put timber companies out of business. Its goal was to preserve enough redwoods that future generations could enjoy them, thus cooperation and negotiation seemed to increase its chances for success. Not that every encounter with logging companies insured cooperation—many remained staunchly opposed to any kind of compromise or negotiation.

Interestingly, the dramatic economic downturn of the Great Depression actually augmented the drive to acquire new forestlands, even as the corresponding drop in timber demand led to a 35 percent decrease in production. As a result, Save-the-Redwoods League and other groups were able to purchase more redwood timberland, including the highly revered groves at Bull Creek and Dyerville Flats, a pristine parcel originally owned by Pacific Lumber.

While the League worked hard to encourage the purchase of more redwood groves, it did not seek help from the federal government. Purchases were still seen as the domain of state/local and private entities. The League even resisted the National Park Service's recommendation that the federal government purchase 18,000 acres on Mill Creek. The League, in conjunction with the Del Norte Lumber Company and the state, was able to purchase 7,000 acres at Mill Creek in 1939. Unfortunately, much of the land the League had hoped to acquire was logged before this could eventually be accomplished.

The first redwood forestland actually acquired by federal funds was a purchase of land located along the Klamath River, but this tract was subsequently scheduled for timber harvest. Ironically, the federal government would not make any other redwood purchases until Redwood National Park was established in 1968.

Pacific Lumber provided jobs for generations of loggers around Humboldt.

However, a significant step was taken when an important lumber company stepped up to the plate and agreed to help promote the preservation of the redwoods. That company was Pacific Lumber, or PL, as it was called.

According to many of those who worked for PL, the company was "never just any lumber company—it was *the* lumber company." Not only large, it dominated the region around Humboldt, and generations of loggers found work in its forests. It was, in truth, a family affair.

According to David Harris in his book *The Last Stand*, Albert Stanwood Murphy, who became president of Pacific Lumber in 1931, instituted two policies that were unique to the logging industry. Murphy had inherited the company from his father, but he, like the Murphys to follow, learned the trade from the bottom up, from working with the men in "hobnailed boots" to moving on to the company's main San Francisco office, where he learned the "ledger side of the business." He was beloved by all who worked for him, especially during the years of the Great Depression, when PL fed "all comers out of its Scotia cookhouse."

The first revamped policy the thirty-nine-year-old Murphy introduced was *how* the company would cut its trees. The accepted method at this time was clear-cutting, which—when the rains came—led to tremendous erosion and devastation. Murphy changed that policy perhaps, in part, because California had enacted a new timber tax incentive that encouraged loggers and logging companies to leave a portion of their harvested timberland untouched. But regardless of his motivation, it had important consequences.

Pacific Lumber's new policy involved "selective cutting." A maximum of 70 percent of a mature stand would be cut, leaving the remaining 30 percent to hold the hillsides intact and help reseed the area. Redwoods reseed easily when conditions are stable. In this way, the forest would not be destroyed, as in years past. In one account it was noted that after PL's Cat (tractors used to haul the lumber out) tracks had grown over, it was hard for the untrained eye to detect that a significant amount of timber had even been cut.

The company's second policy change was also a move to help preserve the redwoods—and that included the pace at which timber would be cut.

Murphy, a third-generation lumber miller, realized that overcutting was not a healthy practice. He recognized that after only seventy years of logging, the California coastal redwoods, which had once covered some two million acres, had been nearly depleted. This new policy he dubbed "sustained yield." So, while other companies might cut indiscriminately, Pacific Lumber would not. Its annual cut would always be limited, no matter what the demand might be.

Clearly, Pacific Lumber's approach was unique, but significant. Until July 1985 both policies—sustained yield and select cut—remained the company's "iron rule."

THE HOSTILE TAKEOVER OF PACIFIC LUMBER

Pacific Lumber was a company that had practiced conservation in its management of redwood timber. Without warning, Warren Murphy and family, who had owned the company since 1863, were suddenly "dethroned" in September of 1985 when Charles Hurwitz and Maxxam, Inc., a Texas corporation, relieved them of their stock holdings in a hostile takeover. Maxxam was known to take over companies and break them apart in order to disperse their assets.

To everyone's shock—even horror—Hurwitz replaced the long-held family practice of sustainable growth policies with a renewed and aggressive form of clear-cutting.

The fight to save the redwoods under PL's control was on. Protestors and activists joined the struggle, hoping to stop the company's destructive timber policies concerning the Headwaters Forest, the largest privately owned ancient redwood forest left. Hurwitz began cutting timber at three times the rate of Pacific Lumber.

Was there any way to curb the cutting?

Many joined the fight to save the Headwaters Forest, not least of which were organizations such as the Sierra Club and Earth First! Even the public's response was fueled against the corporation.

In May 1990 a bomb exploded in the car of Judi Bari, an Earth First! activist who, along with fellow passenger and activist Darryl Cherney, was sent to the hospital. No arrests were initially made, but then Bari was charged with transporting an explosive device until the case was dropped a few months later. She later sued the FBI, and was ultimately successful, but by that time Bari had already passed away from cancer.

In 1998 a tree being cut on PL property struck activist David Chain. He was killed instantly. Though videotape revealed that the loggers had been yelling in the direction of the activists prior to the accident, the company maintained that the loggers were unaware of the protestors' location.

Despite liquidating PL's assets and worker benefits and pensions, Pacific Lumber/Maxxam was $700 million in debt. Pacific Lumber, under Maxxam, filed for bankruptcy in 2007; in 2008 the order for reorganization was signed. The bankruptcy court transferred PL's buildings, mill, and 210,000 acres of its Humboldt forest to Mendocino Redwood Company—a California-based company.

Mendocino Redwood Company, LLC, along with Humboldt Redwood Company, LLC, together now manage about 440,000 acres of forest lands along the northern California coast. Their shared objectives include a high standard of stewardship and environmental practices that will keep the forests in good health. They also have a number of restoration projects underway that reflect the companies' strong stand for good management.

The State Parks Come First

*As I drove through the entrance of the park and beheld the sign which
read "To Be Preserved In A State Of Nature," I knew my life was
to be profoundly changed forever. I knew I had to make this my life.*
—HARRIET "PETEY" WEAVER, FIRST FEMALE
CALIFORNIA STATE PARKS RANGER

BEFORE THE OCTOBER 2, 1968, DEDICATION OF REDWOOD NATIONAL
Park, a number of state parks were established up and down the northern
California coastline; today there are 118 state parks in California, many
of which preserve redwood forestland.

Of these, Jedediah Smith Redwoods State Parks and Del Norte
Coast Redwoods State Parks (both in Del Norte County) along with
Prairie Creek Redwoods State Parks (in Humboldt County)—and with
Redwood National Park—comprise the Redwood National and State
Parks.

The Redwood National and State Parks encompass more than
132,000 acres in Del Norte and Humboldt counties, and though the
parks preserve almost 39,000 acres of old growth forest, most of the acreage is second-growth trees. Some areas along the Mill Creek and Rock
Creek watersheds were logged as recently as 1999.

While not part of Redwood National and State Parks, Humboldt
Redwoods State Park is worth mentioning since it encompasses several
important and historic groves and is one of the more-visited parks in the
northwestern corner of California. It is about thirty minutes south of
Eureka and encompasses over fifty thousand acres, including the Rockefeller Forest at Bull Creek Flat and a series of memorial groves along the

Redwood Highway, such as the Franklin K. Lane Memorial Grove, the Bolling Memorial Grove, and the Children's Forest—a "fairyland" where gifts have been made in memory of children who have died. Four of the coast redwoods that measure over 370 feet tall are here in Humboldt Redwoods State Park as well—encompassed in tracts of virgin redwoods often called the "cathedral groves."

Other groves within Humboldt Redwoods State Park include the grove named for the Native Daughters of the Golden West, the California Federation of Women's Clubs, and the Garden Club of America. There's Dyerville Flat—a stand of especially tall trees, including the Founders' Tree. And running through Humboldt State Park is the incomparable Avenue of the Giants, which wends its way through the majestic redwood forestlands.

Prairie Creek Redwoods State Park was one of the first of the state parks to be established (donated by Zipporah Russ in 1923). Save-the-Redwoods League had early on recognized that Prairie Creek was one of the prime locations and would be ideal park land. Zipporah Russ donated 160 acres of prime canyon land as the first land to be included in the new Prairie Creek Redwoods State Park, in spite of the fact (or perhaps because of it) that her husband had actually been implicated in a land fraud scheme.

According to Save-the-Redwoods League literature, it differs "in character from that of the redwood forest of southern Humboldt County with its heavy 'flats' of virgin redwoods along the river bottoms. The Prairie Creek forest combines both the 'flat' type with the 'slope' type, affording splendid examples of both. The 'slope' timber is unusual in quality, size, and density of stand, and the forest cover very luxuriant."

Located near the small town of Orick and fifty miles north of Eureka, one of the most important aspects of Prairie Creek Redwoods State Park is the grazing herds of Roosevelt elk (*Cervus elaphus roosevelti*). Easily spotted on the broad prairie, known as Elk Prairie, they represent a wildlife conservation success story.

Prairie Creek Redwoods State Park also includes stretches of coastline and beaches, including the 250-foot Gold Bluffs. It was the Save-the-Redwoods League that succeeded in extending the park's boundaries in 1926 and 1931, after acquiring nearly five thousand acres from a large timber company, the Sage Land and Improvement Company. Then, in 1965, Prairie Creek Redwoods State Park acquired a thirty-acre section including Fern Canyon. Today the park encompasses 14,000 acres of old growth coast redwoods. Two renowned redwoods include Big Tree and Corkscrew Tree, with its multiple trunks, which twist round each other.

It's common to spot black bear, Roosevelt elk, bobcats, mountain lions, spotted owls, and marbled murrelets within Prairie Creek Redwoods State Park. One grove located here was named for German forester Carl A. Schenck who, in 1898, founded the Biltmore School of Forestry, the first national institution dedicated to scientific forest management.

During the Depression, a Civilian Conservation Corps camp was established on the prairie and the young men worked to clear debris left behind by the road crews working on the Redwood Highway. They split wood into rail fencing and built the park's visitor center, which features hand-hewn beams and a rock fireplace.

Jedediah Smith Redwoods State Park, located not far from Crescent City, is considered by many to be the most beautiful of all the redwood parks. It was established in 1928 with only a small grove, but in 1939 the state obtained almost seven thousand acres from the Del Norte Lumber Company.

Today's 10,000-acre park boasts some spectacularly sized redwoods. Though perhaps not as tall as many of the redwoods to the south, they are bigger in diameter. Because it has more old growth trees per acre than any other park, Jedediah Smith Redwoods State Park is also considered the most unspoiled of California's redwood parks. It contains a number of important groves, including the National Tribute Grove, which memorializes men and women who served in the armed forces during World War II. There is also the Frank D. Stout Memorial Grove at the confluence of the Smith River and Mill Creek. This small grove is perhaps the most scenic redwood grove in existence, and the huge, straight trees are often described as having a cathedral-like ambiance.

In addition, the Little Bald Hills Trail rises up out of the old growth redwoods to a hilltop pine forest.

South of Jedediah Smith Redwoods State Park is Del Norte Coast Redwoods State Park, which was established in 1925. Stretching from False Klamath Cover to the Foothills southeast of Crescent City, the original designation included only a 157-acre grove dedicated to Henry Solon Graves and incorporates steep cliffs populated with Sitka spruce, flat river canyons, and rocky beaches. Mill Creek and Rock Creek flow in the park. Within six years, the park was expanded by over 2,000 acres. Today the park covers 33,000 acres and extends from the Pacific Ocean on the west into the Mill Creek Basin and the west fork of Mill Creek.

Del Norte Coast Redwoods State Park is the only major redwood park that does not encompass any "lowland redwoods." Instead the park sits atop a steep hillside above the Pacific Ocean, making it often foggy and damp. This area receives the state's heaviest rainfall, up to 70 inches. Because of its weather and climate, rhododendrons thrive here, making it a photographer or artist's "paradise," though not as popular with hikers and recreationists.

Much of the park's Pacific coastline is rocky as well, with a number of cliffs, escarpments, and sea stacks that rise up out of the sea. The often foggy, rough, and undeveloped beaches provide a retreat from the hustle and bustle of the workaday world. In 2002, Del Norte Coast Redwoods Park was expanded with the forty-square-mile purchase of the Mill Creek watershed. The property was bought from Stinson Lumber Company to protect the Jedediah Smith Redwoods from the damage created by earlier upstream logging, which had occurred during the 1970s, '80s, and '90s. Out of the acreage purchased, only a few small old growth redwood stands remained.

Moreover, many of the old dirt and gravel logging roads are now being removed, although some have been designated as trails and are open to the public for hiking, horseback riding, and mountain biking. Other well-known sites in this park include some named features, such as False Klamath Cove, Sister Rocks, and Footstep Rocks.

The Tall Trees Bring
Recognition to the Forest

IT'S HARD TO SAY THAT SOME TREES ARE MORE SIGNIFICANT THAN OTHERS when it comes to the redwoods. Each is a magnificent specimen. At the same time, there have been a number of trees identified—and still being identified—as trees of such size and breadth that explorers and adventurers are drawn to them, almost as if on pilgrimage. Standing in front of these awesome trees is a humbling experience.

Measuring the redwoods has become an enterprise in the last few decades, and, while "redwood explorers" and researchers, such as Dr. Robert Van Pelt and Dr. Steve Sillett, have contributed to the understanding of some of the Redwood National and State Parks' tallest trees, park personnel prefer to underscore the importance of an entire forest ecosystem versus individual trees. Today's scientists are more involved in the study of the parks' forest canopy as well as the effects of climate change on coastal redwoods.

Chris Atkins and Michael Taylor, however, are credited with compiling lists of the tallest redwoods located along the coast in the last few years. The presently known "tallest" redwood is located in Redwood National Park and was first identified by Atkins and Taylor in 2006. Dr. Steve Sillett from California State University at Humboldt climbed this redwood, which was filmed by National Geographic.

In 2013 that tree, Hyperion, was measured and its official measurement was 379.1 feet tall with a diameter of 15.88 feet, making it the tallest of all plant species recorded anywhere in the world. Keeping this in

This Bull Creek redwood specimen stands 345 feet high, but there are more and more trees whose measurements surpass 370 feet.
FRANK PATTERSON, PHOTOGRAPHER

perspective, this means that Hyperion is six stories taller than the Statue of Liberty.

Besides Hyperion, there were Helios and Icarus; before Hyperion was discovered, it was assumed that Helios might be the tallest redwood. All three are located in Redwood National Park, with Icarus and Helios located within the same grove.

In 2014 more than a dozen "Titan" trees were identified as having record-breaking diameters, some greater than twenty feet. In fact, the broadest tree has been measured at twenty-seven feet across, which is the length of two Volkswagen Beetles.

Mario Vaden's writings on the coastal redwoods reveal how much new information has been gathered through the years. Regarding the men who have studied the redwoods, he writes, "To redwood explorers, those [new redwood sightings] were like finding a vein of gold and wondering how deep it went."

Vaden writes, "[Michael] Taylor has discovered at least 50 coast redwoods over 350 feet tall, and co-discovered approximately 100 more over 350 feet with Chris Atkins and Prof. Stephen Sillett, who is the first holder of the Kenneth L. Fisher Chair in Redwood Forest Ecology at Humboldt State University."

Other scientists and adventurers who explored the redwood forests in earlier decades include a number of interesting individuals as well. University of California scientist Paul Zinke and graduate student Allen Stangenberger discovered Dyerville Giant around 1966.

Earlier still, Paul Zahl led a National Geographic expedition in 1963 into what soon became Redwood National Park. Zahl is credited with discovering the "Libby" tree, which measured 367.8 feet; unfortunately 10 feet were broken off the top of the tree during a storm, thus Libby lost its world's tallest tree title. More important is that Zahl's discovery added additional impetus to establish the national park we now know as Redwood National Park.

Dr. Robert Van Pelt, author of *Forest Giants of the Pacific Coast*, along with Dr. Steve Sillett, began exploring Redwood National Park in hopes of finding and measuring some tall trees. In 1998 the pair discovered the "Lost Monarch," in Jedediah Smith Redwoods State Park, which was then tagged the largest redwood.

Within Redwood National Park are four more trees that measure over 370 feet, with new discoveries coming to light each year.

Plants and Animals That Depend
on the Redwoods

Without the scurry and scratch of a chipmunk along the bark or the call of a jay and the flash of its blue, the high mountain and the deep gorge would be cold, dead indeed. The visitor would not linger long after his first comprehensive gaze at awesome scenery if the vista did not include the intimate details of those living things, the plants, the animals that live on them, and the animals that live on those animals.
—GEORGE MELENDEZ WRIGHT, NATIONAL PARK SERVICE,
SERVED FROM 1927–1936

REDWOOD NATIONAL AND STATE PARKS IS A SIGNIFICANT HABITAT FOR many species of plants and animals, including several that are threatened or endangered.

Over two hundred distinct plant species are located within a redwood forest, from more rugged conifers such as Douglas fir and western hemlock to smaller and more fragile plants such as the tiger lily and Pacific bleeding heart. A wide variety of species are found in areas to the north and to the south, which demonstrates how diverse redwood forests can be.

Walking through a redwood forest feels like a journey through some green and exotic landscape, and it's hard not to wonder at the layers of plant life that exist. From the floor where a variety of ferns and other spreading herbs grow, to the shrubs that often bloom with color, to the upper canopies of conifers and redwoods, the forest seems to radiate an "otherworldly" aura.

While some of the notable plant species found among the redwoods actually range from Alaska and the Pacific Northwest down through the northern California coast, other species dominate the central and southern range of California redwoods. The kind of plant life that thrives, however, is dependent on the type of redwood forest landscape in which it's located; the three types of forest include the alluvial-flat forest, the redwood/mixed evergreen forest, and the redwood/Douglas fir forest.

The redwood/mixed evergreen forests are found at upper elevations, while alluvial-flat forests are found along rivers and are populated by old growth timber. The redwood/Douglas fir forests are found adjacent to alluvial-flat forests.

Alluvial plains are largely flat areas created by sediment deposited by one or more rivers coming down from higher elevations; over a long period of time, those rivers, especially in periods of high water and/or floods, leave considerable layers of sediment behind. Oftentimes the level of the river is then raised, which can cause it to meander or seek new, lower paths.

In northern California, the alluvial-flat forest is centered along three major rivers, including the Smith, Klamath, and Eel Rivers. Here the temperatures are mild, the light is diffused, and summer fog predominates; also, the soil is rich, deep, and nutrient-dense, insuring that redwoods grow tall and strong, some even more than 350 feet tall. Redwoods dominate this environment, in particular old growth timber.

Two examples of alluvial-flat communities are located within Humboldt Redwoods State Park: the famous Bull Creek watershed and the Rockefeller Forest. Both of these communities support old growth redwoods, meaning that many of the trees are several hundred years old—and some even older. The area is also characterized by large downed trees, which provide habitat for plants and wildlife. Downed trees can survive for a long time and are an important part of the ecosystem.

The redwood/mixed green forest is characterized by an upper, or "overstory," of redwoods, with some Douglas fir or other conifers mixed in. The next "understory" layer is typically characterized by trees such as tanbark oak and madrone; the shrub layer is characterized by huckleberry and California rhododendron; and the lowest layer is characterized by evergreen violet. This kind of layering protects and supports a healthy forest environment.

The Little Lost Man Creek watershed located in Redwood National Park is an example of a redwood/mixed evergreen forest. Temperatures here fluctuate more dramatically from night to day, and there tends to be less fog and less available moisture on the area's steeper slopes. Finally, summers here are typically very warm.

Over four hundred species of birds live in the redwood forest, including the great blue heron, great egret, common merganser, red-tailed hawk, Cooper's hawk, bald eagle, osprey, American kestrel, western meadowlark, great horned owl, pileated woodpecker, turkey vulture, California valley quail, blue grouse, wild turkey, common robin, western scrub jay, winter wren, chestnut-backed chickadee, varied thrush, and more.

Egrets and herons are known to nest in the tops of redwoods, often pulling off the top branches to use in their nest building. Such trees appear as truncated platforms and come alive as the young birds hatch. One stand of redwoods along the coast has become a relatively well-known "rookery" as the birds, five feet tall with wingspans of four to five feet, have been nesting for nearly a century. It's been estimated that upwards of 180 egrets and 100 herons have used the same grove for their nests. The nesting site was nearly lost to a development many years ago, but the local Audubon Society, after launching a campaign, was able to purchase the property in 1961. Today this site is known as the Audubon Canyon Ranch.

Regarding a somewhat smaller avian resident, one visitor to the redwoods noted, "The tiny Winter Wren, the smallest wren in the West, perhaps the smallest in the world, certainly in the park, lives among the largest trees in the universe, a brown, shadowy mite, difficult to see, flickering in and out of the prostrate boles. Look for him on the ground, never in the high branches."

Another small but intriguing animal that lives in the redwood forest is the banana slug. The slug, which can grow up to ten inches long, thrives in the shady, rainy forest and is related to the snail. It feeds on plants, mushrooms, decaying animals, lichen, and, interestingly enough, poison oak. Its greenish or olive-yellow color acts as camouflage. As banana slugs slither along, they deposit a film of slime, which can be unpleasant for people as they walk along the trails or forest floor. The slug has even become a mascot of sorts for those who enjoy visiting the redwoods!

A variety of plant species also thrives in the heavily shaded redwood landscape. The fern is a non-blooming example of an understory plant that flourishes in a redwood's shaded environment. Ferns have both spreading stems (called rhizomes) and roots and are also found growing along the trunks of downed redwoods, along the cracks found in a redwood trunk's bark, and even up in the canopy; ferns have been found as high up as 270 feet. Surprisingly they are as old, or even older, than the redwoods they depend on, and the variety of ferns is amazing. There are sword ferns, five-finger ferns, deer ferns, licorice ferns, and maidenhair ferns. Botanists have estimated that ferns evolved over three hundred million years ago during the Carboniferous period.

Historically, it's also interesting to note that many of the coast's Native American tribes used ferns. They ate the fern's rhizomes and boiled them for tea. Different stems from various ferns were woven into baskets, adding detail and design to the artisan's craft.

Other small flowering plants that thrive in the moist environment created within the redwood forest include oxalis (also called redwood sorrel), alumroot, wild ginger, delicate Douglas iris, and bleeding heart. Often these plants are found in large patches, almost like a carpet. Less appealing is poison oak, which often wends its way up and around the redwood trunks.

The prairies feature thirty different species of grasses, as well as abundant varieties of wildflowers. Flowering shrubs are less common in redwood forests because of the heavy growth and limited or diffused light. Some examples of flowering shrubs include a variety of dogwood, azalea, rhododendron, and California huckleberry. Flowering hardwood trees include madrone and tanbark oak. Oak trees, including Oregon white oak and California black oak, grow along the edges of the grassy meadows. Like other plant species, oak trees provided abundant amounts of acorns and served as a staple of the local tribes' diet.

Wildlife is often hard to locate in the old growth redwoods, but many species of animals live there. The open grasslands of the Bald Hills host raccoons, rabbits, bobcats, coyotes, and even mountain lions. Hollowed trunks, also called "goosepens," are often home to black bears and bats, while limbs and cavities found in redwood trunks are also home to birds and smaller mammals.

Larger animal life also includes Roosevelt elk. Roosevelt elk, which have seen a significant recovery, are still only found in a few places, including Redwood and Olympic National Parks. But early conservationists quickly grew concerned about the Roosevelt elk when their numbers began declining.

Having helped establish the Boone and Crockett Club in 1887 because he feared the loss of wildlife populations, Theodore Roosevelt initiated a movement to protect elk in the western states. The second-largest member of the deer family, and the largest of the six recognized subspecies of elk in North America, Roosevelt elk bulls can weigh up to 1,200 pounds; females can weigh 600 pounds or more. Because of California's milder winters, elk here do not need to migrate.

Theodore Roosevelt, the twenty-sixth president of the United States, was a great conservationist and outdoorsman who promoted preservation.

With attention turned on their declining populations, the western subspecies, *Cervus elaphus occidentalis*, was named "Roosevelt elk" in President Roosevelt's honor. Unfortunately, their numbers continued to decline as settlers in the region hunted them nearly to extinction. By 1912 reportedly only 126 Roosevelt elk were left in northern California. Finally, on a small stretch of land within Prairie Creek Redwoods State Park, the Save-the-Redwoods League took a stand. They pressed for public awareness and began to raise funds for the species' preservation.

As a result, the recovery of the Roosevelt elk is a success story. Within Redwood National Park, as well as Prairie Creek Redwoods State Park, elk numbers have flourished, and today tourists can view them in many locations; one popular spot is at Elk Prairie and another is at Elk Meadow. Elk are also occasionally spotted along the beach at Gold Bluffs, but take shelter and seek protection in the redwoods.

Clearly, Theodore Roosevelt was the perfect man for his time. In 1901 he became vice president under President William McKinley, then unexpectedly became president when McKinley was shot six months into his presidency. He later won the 1904 presidential election in a landslide

The Boone and Crockett Club

The Boone and Crockett Club was founded by Theodore Roosevelt and a handful of friends in 1887. Concerned with the loss of wildlife populations across the continent, and with them the potential loss of hunting opportunities, it was the first hunter-conservationist organization in North America.

Some of the club's original members, including John C. Merriam, actually helped establish the Save-the-Redwoods League. According to the club's website, over the last 125-plus years the organization has helped restore forest and rangeland habitats and has spawned or supported other wildlife conservation organizations, including the New York Zoological Society (1895), National Audubon Society (1905), Wildlife Management Institute (1911), National Wildlife Federation (1937), Ducks Unlimited (1937), and American Wildlife Conservation Partners (2000). In addition, it champions all of the principal federal land-management agencies, including the US Forest Service, National Park Service, Bureau of Land Management, and US Fish and Wildlife Service.

Today the Boone and Crockett Club, a nonprofit organization, continues its dedication to hunter and conservation ethics and has a strong interest in youth and education as it integrates agriculture and wildlife conservation.

victory. His ambition and fortitude would characterize his presidency and give momentum to the national conservation movement.

Roosevelt's legacy includes a number of accomplishments; more national park landmarks and units are dedicated to his memory than any other American president. In 1903 he visited Yellowstone National Park, the Grand Canyon, and Yosemite, where he and John Muir camped out for three nights. Under the starlit sky, they talked about the protection of forests, Yosemite in particular. And when Roosevelt spoke at the state capitol afterwards, he talked emotionally about the majestic sequoias, which he called "monuments in themselves." Roosevelt was able to use the controversial Antiquities Act to achieve what years of dreaming and hoping had not been able to accomplish.

FISH LIFE AT REDWOODS

Because Redwood National and State Parks border miles of California coastline, they also provide more than 62,000 acres of significant habitat for marine life. Two species of fish that rely on this habitat include chinook and coho salmon.

Salmon is and has been the primary food source of the region's coastal tribes. From earliest times, fish and fishing have played a critical role in Native American cultures; the people depended heavily on fish to eat and to trade, and as an element in native cultural practices and religious rites. Tribes often planned their own movement and settlement around the migration patterns of fish species. When the tribes signed treaties with the US government, relinquishing their traditional and historical lands, many received assurances that they could and would be able to continue their right to hunt, fish, or gather in traditional ways. In reality, fishing rights can vary from tribe to tribe.

However, California's coastal tribes have retained the right to fish, as outlined in this amended ordinance issued by the Yurok Tribal Council in 2007: "The purpose of this Ordinance is to protect the fishery resources and thereby tribal fishing rights by establishing procedures for the conservation of fish stocks and exercise of federally-reserved fishing rights. This Ordinance is intended to allow fishing opportunity to Yurok Tribal

Yurok fisherman fishing with a net for smelt at Trinidad.
PHOTOGRAPH BY EDWARD S. CURTIS, LIBRARY OF CONGRESS

members, while at the same time assuring adequate spawning escapement and the attainment of conservation objectives."

There are at least seventeen distinct runs of chinook salmon in California, and they exhibit diverse patterns that allow them to take advantage of the variety of river and ocean environments. Chinook salmon are "anadromous" fish, where adults migrate upstream to spawn in freshwater streams, while juveniles migrate downstream to the ocean to grow and mature. Time spent in the ocean varies greatly among the different runs.

The southern Oregon and northern California coastal chinook salmon include fall-run chinook in coastal streams from Cape Blanco in Oregon south to the Klamath River in California as well as in Smith River and smaller coastal streams in the Redwood National and State Parks region. Southern Oregon and northern California coastal chinook salmon were proposed for federal listing in 1999, but their listing was determined not warranted. Fall, late-fall, and spring-run chinook spawn and rear in the Trinity River and in the Klamath River upstream of the mouth of the Trinity.

Southern Oregon and northern California coast coho salmon are listed as a threatened species under both federal and state Endangered Species Acts. The decline of coho has been attributed to the loss of suitable habitat and changing climatic factors, including the region's recent drought and poor oceanic conditions that reduce the quality of stream rearing. Human activities have also impacted coho runs; this includes commercial overfishing and the loss or degradation of suitable freshwater, estuarine habitats and/or other land developments.

South of RNSP, one rancher, raised along Bear River, cited the demise of salmon in the 1940s and '50s, as described in *Humboldt Heartland*: "We had lots of salmon in the river when I was young—the late '30s and '40s. Then by the later '40s the fish became more and more scarce and by 1950 they were gone. We always blamed it on to the fishing boats because we could see them anchored off the mouth. The salmon would school up out there before they could come into the river because the lagoon was closed until the first rain came. Logging didn't take place on Bear River until after 1950 so we couldn't blame logging on the demise of the salmon because the salmon were nearly gone before then."

Both the state and federal agencies have proposed and developed coho salmon recovery plans. The recovery actions fall into two categories: habitat-based actions and population-based actions. One plan involves captive rearing, which would include the temporary removal of juvenile coho from Redwood Creek, rearing them to maturity to be released as adults back into their stream of origin.

The Redwood Highway Cuts a Path through the Trees

US Highway 101, also known as the Redwood Highway, is the nation's westernmost federally owned highway. Originally it was nothing more than a series of dirt and gravel wagon roads, and the terrain—rugged, steep, winding, and arduous—made travel up and down the coast of California more than just an exhausting adventure. It could be downright dangerous.

Even in good weather, travel was hard on animals. The hundred-mile stage trip from Willits to Eureka took two days—when the weather was good. Simply put, the land behind the "Redwood Curtain" was tough country, and getting in or out—or even around—was not for the faint of heart. Even going from San Francisco to Eureka was a several-day journey, and if not by stage or wagon, sailing up the coastline was often fraught with danger. Many ships were lost en route.

In 1914 the Northwestern Pacific Railroad completed its link to Humboldt County, and it was celebrated in style. In promoting its Redwood Empire Route, fliers and advertisements promised travelers "every variation of pleasure and recreation, every phase of beauty that the world affords, every charm of climate that the town-weary may seek."

When automobiles arrived on the scene, it was still a rigorous enterprise, but would-be travelers and adventurers were eager to take to the roads, one way or the other.

The building of the Redwood Highway became much more than the construction of just another new roadway. The Redwood Highway, now known as Highways 101 and 199, was an immense undertaking

In the early days, driving the Redwood Highway was an adventure.
FRANK PATTERSON, PHOTOGRAPHER

that literally changed the way politicians, tourists, entrepreneurs, and the average Californian viewed the land of the redwoods. No longer were the redwoods the private "estate" of loggers or local residents; no longer were they locked up in the harsh terrain that encircled and protected them from the outside world, cut off by the rugged Coast Range.

In the early days of motorized travel, the trip from San Francisco to Eureka was at least a three- or four-day journey—again, in good weather—and drivers had to maneuver the ruts and narrow roads, along with the steep curves of the Eel River canyon. While there were fewer than three hundred registered vehicles in California in 1907, by 1910 that number jumped to nearly a thousand. But traveling long distances was a challenge, frequently hampered by weather, poor road conditions, or, more importantly, the lack of acceptable roads.

Although the state highway system actually dates back to 1895, when California took control of the Lake Tahoe Wagon Road (now US Highway 50), the most significant step taken by the state occurred that year when the legislature created a three-person Bureau of Highways to help counties plan and build good roads. The bureau actually traveled to every county during 1895 and 1896, after which it prepared a map of possible state roads. The bureau submitted its recommendations to the governor in 1896.

In 1897 the legislature replaced the Bureau of Highways with the Department of Highways. In the years that followed, a number of new roads were established, or at least drafted.

In 1907 California legislators created the Department of Engineering, which was to oversee and maintain all highways within the state. On the heels of this, the legislature passed the State Highway Act of 1909. The act allowed for bonds to be passed for the acquisition and construction of a system of state highways. The $18 million bond issue, which was ratified by Californians in November 1910, stated, "Under this act the counties pay the interest on state highway bonds, the proceeds of the sale of which are expended within the county." Thus, construction of a three-thousand-mile highway system began in earnest in 1912.

Unfortunately, because the first bond issue did not provide enough funding for the initial wave of roads, a new State Highways Act was passed in 1915 and enacted in 1916. This act provided $12 million for completion of the first roads and an additional $3 million for another 680 miles of new roads.

This series of acts literally paved the way for turning what had been old, oft-abandoned wagon roads into two-lane, reasonably maintained highways. Obviously, as the automobile became America's most popular mode of travel, there was an ever-increasing demand for more and better roads.

Construction of the Redwood Highway was slow at first, especially in the more rugged terrain where workers had to pack in supplies and materials by mule train. Moreover, in a few places the road had to be literally carved out of coastal cliffs, and where it passed through redwood forests, redwoods had to be cut down and hauled off.

As recorded in one account, in late January 1912, Harvey M. Harper and his wife set out in their Model T. Harper was anxious to reach Eureka, where he'd recently purchased a Ford dealership. Even in the driest weather, the trip took nearly four full days to travel from San Francisco to Eureka—and that was if nothing went wrong.

After stalling out on a hillside north of Willits, Mrs. Harper had to hold the Ford with a rope so it would not slide off the hill into the river below, while Harvey walked on ahead, shoveling a path through the mud. The couple finally reached Eureka on February 25, almost a full month later.

As recorded in another account, at Devil's Elbow, a hairpin turn along the Mail Ridge Road on the Eel River, cars had to back up to even negotiate the turn. The Mail Ridge Road, at an elevation of four thousand feet, was the only way to get from Willits to Eureka. Clearly, drivers heading into or through northern California had to battle steep inclines, deep gullies or washouts created by rain and erosion, and narrow passages around cliffs or through dense forests.

Sadly, some traffic issues ended in disaster, as recorded in the June 11, 1913, *San Francisco Call*: "DOCTOR KILLED WHEN AUTO JUMPS GRADE: Dr. Charles W. Mills of Arcata was killed and Dr. E. Hill was seriously injured today when their automobile plunged over grade on Berry's Hill, east of Redwood Creek. The physicians were returning from Horse Mountain. Doctor Mills was at the wheel when the car got beyond control while coming down the hill."

A passable road was finally constructed between Sausalito and Arcata, but the road from Arcata to the California/Oregon border was still years from completion. As reported in the *California Highway Bulletin* in 1916, "The country traversed is in a virgin state, for the most part devoid of wagon roads or even passable trails. The scenery is unsurpassed in California, and the redwood forests, river views and picturesque ruggedness will be a revelation to the tourist."

With the approach of World War I, construction on the Redwood Highway came to an almost complete stop; however, in 1915 the legislature approved the use of convict labor to complete the next stretches of roadway. The convicts were allowed to receive a dollar a day in pay; in addition, for every day worked, they received two days "credit" toward their term. Throughout the war years, convicts were able to keep construction of the highway going. The men worked year-round, six days a week, even in snow and rain.

When completed, the highway would effectively shrink the rugged northern reaches of California by connecting the small coastal communities in counties such as Mendocino, Humboldt, and Del Norte with San Francisco and the Bay Area, as well as with Oregon.

But, without some kind of bridge across the great Klamath River, all traffic came to a halt. Ferries, and sometimes even canoes, were used to haul passengers, cars, and other traffic across the Klamath. The crossing was becoming more and more dangerous, and people wanted something to be done.

The demand for a bridge grew more heated. With more than fourteen thousand registered vehicles in California by 1920, local tourists were flocking to the redwood coast, and during the summer that number was multiplied several times over by out-of-state visitors. However, California's annual state highway fund was only $25 million, and little of it was allocated to the less-populated areas of the state.

In response, the Redwood Highway Association was founded in 1921. By 1925 the group evolved into the Redwood Empire Association, which hoped to develop the entire region economically through the construction of better roads. Attracting tourists and visitors became its primary goal. Incorporating nine counties, the group was able to lobby much more successfully in Sacramento.

The May 1922 *Motor Land* reported, "A bridge over the Klamath is one of the keys to a great wealth of travel from Oregon and the Northwest. Now the inadequate ferry facilities, relying on tide and weather conditions, make the coast trip [to Oregon] one of probabilities rather than certainties."

Even the governor called for the construction of a bridge. After touring the region, Governor Friend Richardson signed the bill approving the Doctor Douglas Memorial Bridge, to be constructed near Requa.

The Douglas Memorial Bridge over the Klamath was finally completed in 1926. Named for Gustave H. Douglas, the bridge had become his dream. Douglas was a devoted doctor who was known to once pump a railroad handcar eighteen miles in order to reach a patient in a remote cabin. After he became a state assemblyman, he pushed for the construction of the bridge. Sadly, he died in office, but his legacy lives on in the majestic bridge that bore his name.

Also noted in the May 1922 *Motor Land*, the newly designated California Redwood Highway "possesses a wealth of scenery, particularly after it reaches the canyon of the Eel River, and it passes through some of the most extensive, and some of the finest groves of redwood trees that the State can boast."

The Douglas Memorial Bridge was to have a major impact on travel to, as well as up and down, California. As reported in Diane Hawk's book, *Touring the Old Redwood Highway, Del Norte County*, "The centuries-old calm of the virgin redwood forest along the Redwood Highway was disturbed last month by the coming of 6,000 (actually 4,000) people from all over the western states to witness the dedication of the newest link of the Redwood Highway—the Douglas Memorial Bridge." This mammoth structure became a watershed event in the opening up of the redwood forests.

The bridge was nearly 1,200 feet long, with five massive arches, and it stood 51 feet above the river. It was a grand bridge, the longest such structure in the state, and its dedication was a grand event. Governors Friend W. Richardson of California and Walter M. Pierce of Oregon attended. As noted in one report, "Contestants from Hupa and Requa competed in an Indian stick game. A special highlight was 'an exhibit of all the wild flowers in Del Norte County [that] was staged upon the bridge, and was beautiful.'" Douglas's widow and son were present for the dedication, after which lines of waiting cars and trucks crossed the Klamath River unaided.

The bridge's construction meant that at long last, travelers could drive over four hundred miles, from Sausalito to Crescent City, without having to be ferried over the river. But more than that, with the opening of the bridge, the road into the redwoods was established and the lure of the majestic forests along the coast was ignited.

Tourist attractions began popping up all along the highway. The first motels, called "auto courts," were built, along with campgrounds, restaurants, and garages and gas stations. Redwood attractions such as the Stump House and drive-through trees, the more elegant Eureka Inn and Benbow Inn, and even the "Trees of Mystery" lured families and adventurers farther north. Vacationing became a novel event, and its importance in the lives of people grew along with the improved roads.

President Calvin Coolidge endorsed the newly developing highway system, stating, "Highways should continue to have the interest and support of the government. Everyone is anxious for good highways. I have made a liberal proposal in the budget for the continuing payment to the states by the federal government of its share for this necessary public improvement. No expenditure of public money contributes so much to the national wealth as building good roads."

The Golden Gate Bridge Increases Travel to the Redwoods

One of the most significant events to impact the Redwood Highway and provide access to the redwoods was the May 27, 1937, opening of the Golden Gate Bridge. The event was cause for celebration in San Francisco and up and down the coast, as announced in the *Sausalito News* on April 23, 1937: "BRIDGE FIESTA HOLIDAY: A business holiday throughout the Redwood Empire on the opening day of the Golden Gate Bridge Fiesta May 27 has been urged by the Santa Rosa Chamber of Commerce. On that day, the Golden Gate Bridge will be thrown open to public inspection for the first time, yet no vehicles will be allowed." In addition, "Market Street and other main thoroughfares of San Francisco will resemble a grove of redwoods during the Golden Gate Bridge Fiesta period, May 27 to June 2. The trolley poles and electric light poles will be wrapped in redwood bark and topped with boughs of redwoods."

Before the bridge's construction, approximately 1.5 million cars traveled the coastal highway north of San Francisco annually. Ten years after its construction, more than 7.5 million vehicles crossed it to travel into the northernmost regions of California. The Golden Gate is still, no doubt, the signature landmark for the state of California—but, just as importantly, it operated as the gateway to the redwood empire.

This acknowledgment of the role of the federal government was important since counties carried the weight of putting together the monies required to build and develop new roads.

Obviously, the construction of the Redwood Highway attracted thousands of new visitors to the rugged redwood region, as noted by the *Sausalito News* in an October 16, 1936, article: "Good roads, of course, are not the entire attraction as we all know; it is our redwood trees and unmatchable scenic coast with the nearby valleys of pastoral beauty that make this Redwood Highway the most noted automobile and stage bus route in the west."

And as Arcata Commissioner Louis Everding, of the California Highway Commission, acknowledged, "The completed road will open a section of primal forest along the beautiful Smith River, through a country heretofore inaccessible except on foot or horseback."

This exposure led to more calls for increased protection for acres of remaining redwoods, as well as an increased demand for exploiting one of the world's most fabulous resources. As the road became a popular thoroughfare, motels, curio shops, and eateries were built along its sides; redwood-themed attractions were also built, including the "World's Largest Redwood Tree Service Station" in Ukiah, the "One-Log House" in Phillipsville, and the "Trees of Mystery" near Requa.

The Redwood Highway eventually became part of US Highway 101. Over time the road was improved and modernized. In the 1950s there was a push to expand the road, which required removing a number of trees within Humboldt Redwoods State Park. Newton B. Drury, chief of the California Division of Beaches and Parks, and others initiated protests voicing strong objection and indignation. The outcry made a difference, and a forty-four-mile bypass was approved, saving the threatened groves.

Redwood National Park Is Established

The story of our national parks is the story of America. It is the story of our never-ending struggle to live up to the democratic ideal that these parks belong to all of us. Most of all, it is the story of our determination to protect and preserve those places that define our history and nourish our collective soul.

—IRA S. HIRSCHFIELD, PRESIDENT,
EVELYN AND WALTER HAAS, JR. FUND

CLEARLY, THERE WAS SERIOUS PUBLIC SUPPORT FOR THE ESTABLISH-ment of parks that would protect the redwoods as early as the mid-1800s. Even President Abraham Lincoln approved historic legislation when he signed the Yosemite Grant Act in 1864, which protected Yosemite Valley and Mariposa Grove. After that, calls for protection of the nation's greatest landforms and landscapes were inevitable.

In 1879 Secretary of the Interior Carl Schurz called for the creation of a national redwood park. He proposed that the President "be authorized to withdraw from sale or other disposition an area at least equal to two townships [46,080 acres] in the coast range in the northern, and an equal area in the southern portion of the state."

On the heels of this, President Grover Cleveland issued an executive order in 1886 that removed ten townships from settlement around Crater Lake in Oregon. Then in 1890, Sequoia, Yosemite, and General Grant national parks were established; these parks protected giant sequoia groves in the Sierra Nevada. The move to protect important landforms had begun.

President Benjamin Harrison then signed the Forest Reserve Act into law in 1891. This law set aside thirteen million acres in forest reserves, including the Sierra Forest Reserve, which protected most of the forestland and watersheds located in the central and southern Sierra Nevada range.

Ironically, with all of this activity, the only national park dedicated to redwood preservation remained the 295-acre Muir Woods National Monument in Marin County—a park created by the private donation of William Kent.

Then, in the September 16, 1899, issue of the *San Francisco Call*, it was reported:

STANFORD UNIVERSITY: The United States Department of Agriculture is desirous of obtaining four Stanford students to do work studying the forestry in Humboldt County. Their chief study will be the magnificent redwood trees, known to scientists as the Sequoia sempervirens. The Government is desirous of finding how the extinction of this species of tree may be prevented. The lumbermen of the northern part of the State are also interested in this work and donate $1000 to help defray the expenses of the expedition. A party of Yale students did similar work among the spruce timber of the same county last summer.

In 1904, President Theodore Roosevelt also expressed his approval for setting aside a tract of California redwood land for protection under the federal government.

Other efforts to establish a national redwoods park were attempted in 1911, 1912, and 1914. However, none of these initial efforts were successful. Few in Congress or others on a national level felt compelled to take up the cause in spite of the desire by so many to preserve the mammoth trees.

As chronicled in previous chapters, undoubtedly, the most important catalysts in the movement to save California's redwoods were the Sempervirens Club and the Save-the-Redwoods League, as well as the Boone and Crockett Club, Sierra Club, and others.

Establishment of the
National Park Service

Although national parks had begun to be designated in the second half of the nineteenth century, and national monuments (by presidential decree) in the early part of the twentieth century, each park or monument was managed individually or, occasionally, by the US Army. Beginning in 1911, Senator Reed Smoot of Utah and Representatives William Kent and John E. Raker of California supported bills to establish the National Park Service, under which all parks and monuments would be listed.

On December 6, 1915, the Sixty-fourth Congress of the United States of America passed the National Park Service Organic Act (or simply the "Organic Act"). It read: "AN ACT to establish a National Park Service (NPS), and for other purposes. . . . Be it enacted by the Senate and House of Representatives of the United States of America in Congress assembled, that there is hereby created in the Department of the Interior a service to be called the National Park Service, which shall be under the charge of a director, who shall be appointed by the Secretary."

President Woodrow Wilson signed the act into law on August 25, 1916, and the first National Park Service director selected to serve was Stephen Mather.

Additionally, the National Park Service General Authorities Act of 1970 was passed as an amendment to the National Park Service "Organic Act" of 1916. The amendment included the following language:

> Congress declares that the National Park Service, which began with establishment of Yellowstone National Park in 1872, has since grown to include superlative natural, historic, and

According to many, the creation of any redwood national park was stymied by the conflict between private rights and public domain, principally because redwoods were seen as a resource and economic commodity as well as a symbol of great intrinsic and environmental value.

recreation areas in every major region of the United States, its territories and island possessions; that these areas, though distinct in character, are united through their inter-related purposes and resources into one national park system as cumulative expressions of a single national heritage; that, individually and collectively, these areas derive increased national dignity and recognition of their superb environmental quality through their inclusion jointly with each other in one national park system preserved and managed for the benefit and inspiration of all the people of the United States; and that it is the purpose of this Act to include all such areas in the System and to clarify the authorities applicable to the system.

Finally, the Redwood Act (also called the Redwood amendment) was a 1978 amendment to the US National Park Service General Authorities Act of 1970. It helped clarify both the 1970 act and the original National Park Service Organic Act of 1916. The following language was added to the 1970 act:

Congress further reaffirms, declares, and directs that the promotion and regulation of the various areas of the National Park System, as defined in section 1c of this title, shall be consistent with and founded in the purpose established by section 1 of this title [the Organic Act provision quoted above], to the common benefit of all the people of the United States. The authorization of activities shall be construed and the protection, management, and administration of these areas shall be conducted in light of the high public value and integrity of the National Park System and shall not be exercised in derogation of the values and purposes for which these various areas have been established, except as may have been or shall be directly and specifically provided by Congress.

Historically, nearly all redwood acreage was already in the hands of private lumbering companies by the 1890s, even as the federal government became involved in the establishment of parks. The accessibility and affordability of acquiring those private lands was seen as an insurmountable challenge.

In 1946, when California congresswoman Helen Gahagan Douglas proposed a national park, her proposal called for a 2.8-million-acre tract of land to be named the Franklin Delano Roosevelt Memorial National Forest. Her plan, a comprehensive one, would encompass the entire northern California region from Sonoma County to the Oregon border. She also proposed that logging be permitted, although logging companies would have to incorporate selective cutting and sustained yield practices.

Opposition for Douglas's proposal came from many fronts. First, Del Norte and Humboldt Counties resisted because 90 percent of their lands would be subject to federal regulation and jurisdiction. Opposition also came from a few other governmental agencies and the Save-the-Redwoods League. Even after a revised bill was proposed in 1949, opposition remained strong, and the bill was quickly scrapped.

As the movement to save the redwoods continued, its focus soon became a total preservation of old growth groves without accommodating logging on any level. At the same time, the post–World War II years brought on an economic boom, including a tremendous demand for lumber and timber products. Returning soldiers were anxious to find work wherever they could, and logging was an industry looking for workers. The rich timbered areas of Prairie Creek and Redwood Creek offered loggers a rich reward.

Del Norte County, hurt by the economic spiral of the 1930s, saw a rapid growth of new mills; in a short period of time, there were more than twenty-five mills operating in the area. The logging industry had been revitalized, and as logging technology improved, access to less accessible forest areas also improved. That led to a huge jump in logging the big trees.

By the 1950s mills were stacking up more than a billion board feet of lumber every year; that amount of cutting continued until the mid-1970s. By the end of the 1950s, only 10 percent of the Pacific coastal redwoods remained uncut.

However, according to Betts and Foster, "public perceptions began to change in the 1950s as aggressive logging operations were undertaken on both private and national forest lands." They add, "Not until the 1950s did public interest in forestry issues begin to make itself felt through the advocacy of various conservation organizations. The Sierra Club and the Izaak Walton League expressed dissatisfaction with the Forest Practice Act and lobbied for the protection of resource values other than timber production, such as watersheds, wildlife, recreation, and aesthetics."

One hopeful sign that a national redwood park might prove possible, however, occurred in 1961, when the federal government allocated funds for the purchase of the Cape Cod National Seashore parkland.

This was the spark conservationists needed.

However, even though the Save-the-Redwoods League, the National Geographic Society, the Sierra Club, and other organizations continued to work for the idea, it wasn't until 1963 that Secretary of the Interior Stewart Udall announced his plan to initiate a proposal for a national redwood park. President Lyndon B. Johnson supported the plan in 1964—although still no site was selected.

Unfortunately, with the 1960s came a new era of logging; in 1961 the Arcata Redwood Company received permission to clear-cut eight hundred acres of old growth groves located along the Redwood Highway in Humboldt County. Until that time, selective cutting had been the predominate practice in California. Then, in 1959, a storm blew down a number of redwoods in selective cut areas of Humboldt County; as a result, Arcata Redwood Company began to question the practice. The company's forester proposed clear-cutting—followed by aerial seeding—a practice used in the Pacific Northwest Douglas-fir region. The Board of Forestry approved a plan to clear-cut 835 acres in 1960. In a 1961 report, "no problems" appeared to exist, in spite of the fact that some of the cutting was in close view of adjacent to the Redwood Highway north of Orick.

On the heels of this, other timber companies began requesting permission to clear-cut their timber reserves. In the years that followed, more than 140 companies submitted plans involving nearly 170,000 acres of redwoods. Simpson Timber Company submitted fifty of these plans.

There seems little doubt that the increased use of clear-cutting dramatically impacted the public's view of logging.

Not only was the land being logged, it was being logged at a pace that was controversial and unsustainable. Many began to raise the alarm, and the need to secure uncut redwood forestlands became apparent;

unfortunately, large tracts of private virgin land were becoming harder to locate and harder to purchase. In addition, with the increased demand for lumber, land prices were skyrocketing.

In 1966 the contemporary struggle for a national park began in earnest. An extensive study conducted by the National Park Service, with funds donated by the National Geographic Society, proposed three different locations to be considered for a park, and all three proposals centered on the Redwood Creek watershed, fifty miles north of Eureka, California, near Orick.

Orick, located halfway between Trinidad and Requa, is now the official gateway to Redwood National Park. Sitting along the banks of Redwood Creek, it was originally a Yurok Indian village but was settled in the 1870s and went through several name changes in that time, including Orekw and Oreq, and finally, Orick. As to its definition, many claim it means "mouth of the river." Others suggest it means "home of the driftwood."

At first sight, it is hard to comprehend that this slip of water— Redwood Creek, which wends its way past Orick—is one of the major streams of the Redwood Belt and home to some of the tallest trees. It travels sixty-seven miles to the sea, running parallel to the Mad River and the lower Klamath. The creek traverses ranch and pastureland and through prairies. Its largest tributaries include Lacks Creek, Minor Creek, Devil's Creek, and Bridge Creek, while countless smaller streams also feed it. Finally, Prairie Creek, which swells with the waters of Lost Man and Little Lost Man Creeks, meets Redwood Creek near Orick.

The redwoods here are tall, some over 350 feet. Along the ridgetops grow more giants; at these higher elevations, there are also fir and spruce and hemlock.

As beautifully penned by Peggy Wayburn in *The Last Redwoods and the Parkland of Redwood Creek*:

> *The once forested flats at the mouth of Redwood Creek were cleared long since, and burned—perhaps a hundred years ago—for pastureland and the building of Orick, a stage stop along the Redwood Highway. But the great groves upriver were off the beaten track.*

*They stood while other grand forests went down, the forests of the
Salmon, the Elk, the Ah Pah, the Mad, and the accessible reaches of
the Klamath, the Smith, and the Eel. The logging of Redwood Creek
waited for the 1940s, and did not really get into swing until the '50s.
So great was the volume on a single acre of its forest land that logging
progressed slowly, even with the modern equipment that lets two men
bring down a redwood tree in an hour. It was the country's great good
fortune that the topography of Redwood Creek helped to spare the
superlative trees and groves growing there—the tallest known tree,
and many others of record size.*

She goes on to note, "Although the Park Service study correctly
identified Redwood Creek as the proper site for a great national park,
its recommendations for the size of the park fell far short of the ideal."

While the National Park Service pushed for a national park encompassing about 53,000 acres, the Sierra Club outlined a proposal that
encompassed 90,000 acres, and this proposal was the one included in a
joint House-Senate bill. More than fifty members of Congress eagerly
supported the bill.

As the debate over the proposal grew more heated, however, it was
clear that the government's position had suddenly changed. Rather than
supporting the more expansive Sierra Club proposal, the director of the
National Park Service, along with the undersecretary of the interior, tes-
tified *against* any park site located along Redwood Creek. Instead they
pushed for a smaller park, to be located along Mill Creek—a location
which would only protect 7,500 acres of virgin trees and where many of
the state redwood parklands were already being preserved.

Why the about-face? What had happened to alter the course of
events? Was it the result of pressure being exerted by logging interests
who wanted to log off the timber along Redwood Creek? Or was it because great sums of money would have to be spent to purchase the private
lands involved in securing the larger location? Remarks later made by
the secretary of the interior gave rise to critical reflection: "We wanted to
pick a park," he said, "not a fight."

For all intents and purposes, however, the National Park Service's attempt to waylay the larger proposal backfired: In 1968 President Lyndon B. Johnson signed a park bill preserving forestlands along Redwood Creek, clearly rejecting the Mill Creek proposal. Moreover, the bill authorized $92 million to be spent on the purchase of private lands in order to protect the designated site.

Unexpectedly, the bill also included a compromise, and in the end called for 58,000 acres of Redwood Creek timberland to be purchased. There was no "buffer zone" included in the proposal, nothing that would protect the watershed.

The newly established national park included only a narrow strip of land along Redwood Creek, including some of the finest groves growing there; it also included some additions to Jedediah Smith Redwoods State Park, taking in thirty-two miles of coastline. Finally, it included three already-designated state parks to become part of the national park: Del Norte Coast Redwoods, Prairie Creek Redwoods, and Jedediah Smith

Lady Bird Johnson and the Lady Bird Johnson Memorial Grove

Claudia Alta Taylor "Lady Bird" Johnson was born in Karnack, Texas, in 1912. As an infant, the family's nurse declared she was as "purty as a ladybird," and the name stuck. In fact, Lady Bird became her official name. Following the assassination of President John F. Kennedy, Lady Bird became the First Lady in 1963 as the wife of Lyndon B. Johnson, thirty-sixth president of the United States. As First Lady, she started a capital beautification project, Society for a More Beautiful National Capital, which involved the planting of millions of flowers. She often stated, "Where flowers bloom, so does hope." She worked extensively with the American Association of Nurserymen to protect wildflowers and helped launch the planting of them along highways.

She also became the first president's wife to work openly for specific legislation, in particular the Highway Beautification Act, which was thereafter dubbed "Lady Bird's Bill." In addition, she

Redwoods. With $92 million in funds to accomplish the purchase, the compromise was accepted.

Again, penned by Peggy Wayburn, "Left out of the present park [were] the forests that still sweep the slopes above Emerald Mile. Left out [was] the only mountain in the redwood region still almost covered by virgin redwood forest. Left out [were] Bridge Creek, Devil's Creek, and most of McArthur Creek and the small superlative watershed of Skunk Cabbage Creek where logging [had] already begun."

She concluded, "These areas should be included in the only Redwood National Park the world will ever have. If they are not, the park may well suffer something like the fate of the Rockefeller Forest on Bull Creek: logging upstream from the park could well make the river as dangerous as Bull Creek was when its floods toppled hundreds of big redwood presumed safe. The scenic fringe of trees along the river, included in the present park, would be subject to catastrophic blowdown were the forest behind logged."

worked to beautify the nation's highways by promoting fewer billboards and the planting of roadside areas. She was active in civil rights and protecting the environment, and supported Head Start. She was the first First Lady to employ a personal press secretary and chief of staff.

Mrs. Johnson visited Redwood National Park in 1968, prior to the park's official designation by Congress. The park was established under President Johnson's administration after several years of negotiation and compromise, but was not formally dedicated until after Richard Nixon took office.

In 1969 President Nixon dedicated the Lady Bird Johnson Memorial Grove in her honor. Reverend Billy Graham provided the benediction.

After being introduced by President Nixon, who acknowledged the tremendous work she'd done for conservation, Lady Bird spoke. She said, "Conservation is indeed a bipartisan business because all of us have the same stake in this magnificent continent. All of us have the same love for it and the same feeling that it is going to belong to our children and grandchildren and their grandchildren."

Lady Bird and President Johnson stand with President Nixon and his wife at the dedication of the Lady Bird Johnson Memorial Grove dedication.
AP IMAGES, USED WITH PERMISSION

Clearly, the decision was controversial, and neither side was particularly pleased with the outcome even though, to some extent, it was a win for conservationists.

Most timber companies opposed the new park and continued to log private lands neighboring the park in spite of the conservationists' concerns over likely erosion and the loss of virgin timber. The Sierra Club and others immediately raised the alarm as logging continued where the park's boundary meandered along the waterway in a winding 7.5-mile corridor called "The Worm," and they pushed for the government to assert its authority over Redwood Creek's upland watershed. Conservationists also pushed the government to begin further negotiations with the logging companies in the hope they would relinquish more land.

According to Edward F. Martin in his report, titled "The California Forest Practice Program: 1976 Through 1988" (written in 1989), "The creation in 1968 of a 58,000+ acre Redwood National Park left very few people happy. . . . Perhaps only the timber companies in the region could be considered to have been slightly grateful; they had faced the prospect of having even more of their lands taken for park purposes."

Two considerations became apparent: 1) 58,000 acres was not enough to justify "national park status;" and 2) the area was still being threatened by nearby and adjoining timber harvests. In the minds of those concerned, the park had been a compromise, and—ironically enough—the tallest known redwood trees, which many fought to have protected, were not even located within the official park's boundaries. They were located in that piece of property known as "The Worm." The strip was only a quarter mile wide on either side of Redwood Creek.

The lands adjacent to the park were owned by Arcata Lumber Company, Louisiana-Pacific Corporation, and Simpson Timber Company—with Louisiana-Pacific owning most of the old growth timber. These lands were upstream and steep, which made them less stable and subject to erosion. As a result, threatened trees of substantial size were now subject to harvesting and the silt created by cutting trees within the drainage could prove devastating.

While pressure mounted for enlarging Redwood National Park, demands for increased regulation of logging near The Worm were also raised. The 1968 Redwood National Park Act contained provisions authorizing the Secretary of the Interior to enter into agreements with the adjoining landholders; for a number of reasons those agreements were never signed by the secretary. The companies, however, did respect the agreements.

Then, in 1975, the Sierra Club filed a lawsuit against the Department of the Interior, demanding that a copy of a report earlier undertaken by the Department of the Interior be released, as required by the Freedom of Information Act, but the government refused to give up the information, and in short order, a court ruled in favor of the Sierra Club. The government was forced to relinquish the study and its results. The study revealed that extensive logging in the areas just outside the park's boundaries had caused massive erosion to the fragile Redwood Creek watershed.

According to James B. Wheeler, "There was so much erosion that the creek bed actually rose 10 to 20 feet in places."

Still, the government's federal budget office refused to consider any additional expenditures or purchases of land located within the Redwood Creek watershed. Instead, the Department of the Interior, including the National Park Service, authorized a second study in 1973. This time the study would include geologic data as well.

Meanwhile, the National Park Service entered into talks with the three large companies logging inside the "buffer zone"—the same area identified as critical by the 1972 Interior Department study.

In 1974, the Natural Resources Defense Council filed a lawsuit against the State Board of Forestry and several companies undertaking timber projects near Redwood National Park. On January 14, 1975, in a landmark ruling, Judge Arthur B. Broaddus of the Humboldt Superior Court ruled that the 1973 Forest Practice Act must abide by the requirements of the California Environmental Quality Act; Environmental Impact Reports (EIRs) would be needed for timber operations.

The first Forest Practice Act (FPA), which had been enacted in 1945, had provided rules by which the harvesting of timber on private lands in California was regulated. With this first act, however, the legislature required only that any person intending to cut "merchantable" timber must first notify the state forester.

Judge Broaddus's decision stunned those in the timber industry and had a profound impact on the future of timbering and forestry.

In the subsequent California Legislature's re-enactment of the FPA, the act was revised, clearly revealing the public's growing interest in fish and wildlife conservation, as well as the sustainability of the forestry industry itself. The new law enacted strict regulations on logging and also contained provisions that timber harvest plans for commercial operations must be prepared by Registered Professional Foresters (RPFs). According to Edward Martin's 1989 report, "These foresters would have greater responsibility for protecting resources."

Meanwhile, the National Park Service and other groups urged the Board of Forestry to enact its own special regulations to help protect the park and considered a set of regulations suggested by state forester Larry Richey. However, the board declined to pass any resolution authorizing a set of rules, but did "direct the state forester to exercise discretionary authority to impose the rule improvements he had proposed." The suggestion was that he would act on a "case by case" basis, or as needed. And, while the California Department of Forestry (CDF) did give consideration to timber plans submitted, few were denied; on the other hand, the timber companies did comply with the extra protections that had been written into their plans.

Such was the tenor of the times: Back and forth went accusations while the logging companies harvested timber on their privately owned lands, and by 1977, the issue exploded on the national scene. Both President Carter and the new secretary of the interior, Cecil Andrus, asked the timber companies to accept a voluntary moratorium on cutting any more timber on those lands that were now being considered for purchase in the latest bill introduced by Phil Burton and Alan Cranston.

Asserting its right to log, one firm, Arcata National Corporation, began cutting along another major stream, Skunk Cabbage Creek, on the first day of the 1977 logging season. Immediately, Secretary Andrus seized thirty-five acres of Arcata's lands with funds provided by Save-the-Redwoods League—an action sanctioned by the original park bill. The tide had turned. The public, as well as Congress, was aware of the critical and tenuous position the redwoods along Redwood Creek now faced. Even the Eureka *Times-Standard* wrote: "If there was one area of private land surrounding the Redwood National Park which was guaranteed to spark action, immediate action, by conservation groups and the federal government, it was the Skunk Cabbage Creek area. . . . The Secretary of the Interior was not only empowered but obligated to acquire additional lands, on a small scale, both for viewshed protection and protection of the existing park."

In 1977, the three major logging companies whose operations posed such danger to the park's health signed an agreement that allowed

California's attorney general to inspect their lands as well as review their companies' timber harvest plans (THPs). As a result, a pending lawsuit filed by the Attorney General was dropped.

Today's FPA requires that anyone seeking to harvest timber must submit a timber harvest plan that's been prepared by a state-registered professional forester and submitted to the State Department of Forestry [CDF] for its review and approval. In addition, the public has an opportunity to review and comment on the proposed timber harvest plan.

About this time, several bills were introduced into Congress regarding the expansion of Redwood National Park. One bill, introduced by Phillip Burton of California, in 1977 called for enlarging the park to include 74,000 acres—nearly the whole Redwood Creek watershed. The Sierra Club supported this proposal.

Another proposal only addressed expanding the park by 21,000 acres; however, this version never found a sponsor.

In the end, President Carter and his administration introduced H.R. 8641 and in the Senate, S. 1976; initially both of these bills contained provisions that gave the federal government control over private lands, but those provisions were deleted before the bills passed. At the same time, as noted by Edward F. Martin in his report, they both contained "unprecedented provisions to assist persons who might suffer displacement from their jobs as a result of park expansion. Organized labor sought and won these concessions."

While these bills were being pursued, both Arcata Redwood Company and Louisiana-Pacific Corporation filed THPs that would impact the proposed acreage identified in the legislation. CDF denied the proposed plans; the companies appealed to the Board of Forestry.

The hearing on the proposed timber harvests was held in May 1977. After long debate about who had authority over the companies' right to harvest the timber and the uncertain future regarding the park's proposed expansion, the board voted 6–3 to uphold two of the denials and 5–4 to uphold a third. The motions, according to Martin's report, "included the statement that there would be no prejudice to resubmission of the plans after 180 days. Presumably, this would give Congress enough time to make up its mind about the expansion."

On the heels of this, more THPs were submitted, denied, then appealed, but each denial was upheld. As tension over appeals and denials continued, President Carter signed the Redwood Park Expansion Bill on March 27, 1978, adding 48,000 acres to the park and providing $359 million for the acquisition of those lands, as well as for any necessary rehabilitation of the acreage that had suffered under clear-cutting. To appease the logging communities, an additional $40 million was provided for the loss of jobs and/or retraining for those loggers who were forced to leave the area or seek a new vocation. Unfortunately the funds were not released in a timely manner, and many loggers were justifiably angered and embittered by the delays.

Reaction to the expansion was split. While many viewed it as a victory, some saw it as a strong-arm tactic by the government. As expressed by the president of Arcata's timber division, "I don't think [the environmentalists] will ever stop. I believe they will keep coming back until they have everything so tied up no one will be able to continue operating."

And because of limits imposed by the 1978 bill, the park was not allowed to purchase additional property. Once more, beginning in the 1980s and continuing into the '90s, it had to rely on donations of additional tracts of land.

In 2000 the Save-the-Redwoods League was able to purchase about two hundred acres of old growth along Mill Creek, which, thankfully, "had an incredibly stable geological makeup, versus Redwood Creek, which was highly erodible."

Redwood National and State Parks now protects approximately 110,332 acres of land, including nearly 40,000 acres of old growth trees and 51,000 acres of second-growth trees. Redwood National Park itself encompasses 75,452 acres and roughly 40 percent of the remaining old growth redwoods (approximately 19,640 acres of old growth timber), but is, in fact, one of the smaller national parks and one of the later parks to be designated. In contrast, Yellowstone National Park, created in 1872, spans 2,219,789 acres, encompassing rivers, lakes, canyons, and mountains.

Thankfully, the early efforts of conservationists effectively spurred the political arm of the government into action, although it took a number of years and a number of attempts before a park was finally established.

Today Redwood National Park is a park of broad differences, with altitudes ranging from sea level to 3,100 feet. Although it's famous for its massive groves of old growth and second-growth redwood trees, it also includes forty to fifty miles of rugged Pacific coastline, with its northern-most boundary beginning only a few miles south of Crescent City and the Oregon border. Founded in 1853, Crescent City possesses a good harbor and is a popular fishing port, both commercially and recreation-ally. It is the county seat and only incorporated city in Del Norte County. As the name implies, it was named for its crescent-shaped stretch of sandy beach south of the city. A National Park Service visitor center is located here, along with the park's official headquarters.

Redwood National Park and its three sister state parks boast three major rivers and their watersheds. Establishment and maintenance of this park has been a significant achievement. Truly, it is the last stand of the giant redwood: Since the expansion in 1978, at least half of all re-maining old growth redwoods are now contained within the boundaries of Redwood National and State Parks.

The Story of Fire in the Forest

But clouds bellied out in the sultry heat, the sky cracked open with a crimson gash, spewed flame—and the ancient forest began to smoke. By morning there was a mass of booming, fiery tongues, a hissing, crashing, howling all around, half the sky black with smoke, and the bloodied sun just barely visible.

— YEVGENY ZAMYATIN, *THE DRAGON: FIFTEEN STORIES*

FOR DECADES THE SIGNIFICANCE OF FIRE IN THE REDWOOD FORESTS HAS not been thoroughly understood. According to Peter Brown and William Baxter, in their 2003 report, "Fire History in Coast Redwood Forests of the Mendocino Coast, California":

We reconstructed fire history in old growth coast redwood (Sequoia sempervirens) stands along an ocean-to-inland gradient in Jackson Demonstration State Forest on the Mendocino Coast in northern California, USA. Fire history was reconstructed for the past two to four centuries using fire scars recorded in tree rings. Surface fires were frequent disturbances in all stands prior to the early twentieth century. Composite mean fire-free intervals aggregated within stands varied from 6 to 20 years, and point mean fire-free intervals averaged within trees varied from 9 to 20 years. Fires ceased in the early 20th century coincident with the advent of organized fire suppression efforts beginning in the 1930s.

Clearly, fire is an integral element of a healthy environment. Plants and animals have learned to adapt, and even to require, natural wildfire.

Consequently, fire management has begun undergoing changes, especially as studies and archaeological evidence demonstrate that even tribes up and down the coastal region used fire regularly and frequently to manipulate their environment, in addition to the natural fires that occurred over the eons.

According to the Save-the-Redwoods website on fires, Steve Norman, a researcher with the US Forest Service, has conducted research on northern forest fire patterns that "led him on a quest to unravel the history of the forest. Lightning strikes could naturally set forests ablaze, but the Tolowa Native American Indians are thought to be the primary source of ignitions in the region before 1850. The Tolowa and similar tribes burned forests annually to encourage a strong harvest of the major food source, acorns, since frequent fires kept down infestations of worms and weevils."

The tribes learned to maintain their tanoak groves through the use of fire: Low-lying fire helped reduce weevils and reduced the amount of dry material that could accumulate and cause greater fire danger that could threaten the trees themselves.

Larger areas were frequently burned to improve hunting conditions and food-gathering opportunities. Burning the forest increased and improved habitat for deer and made hunting large game easier. Burning prairies helped scorch grasshoppers that the tribes used for food, while also controlling the fuel load created by accumulated grass and other dry matter; it also improved the grasslands where materials for basket-making were collected.

Because grassland burns more readily than forest and low-lying shrubs, a ground fire moving through it will only lightly heat the underlying soil. In most grasslands, fire is actually an important method of helping recycle nutrients through decomposition, thus the use of fire by tribes was an efficient and effective way of improving habitat. Yurok Archaeological Field Coordinator Robert McConnell notes, "Our people did a better job managing fire than people do today."

As noted by George Gibbs in his September 1851 journal entry of the Reddick McKee expedition:

The last part of our march led us into a thick redwood forest, upon a mountain, through which we were obliged to cut our trail, the ground being covered with underbrush and fallen timber. A fatiguing climb and an excessively bad descent brought us again to the South Fork. On the other side was a small prairie of about eighty acres, from which however, the grass was mostly burnt. . . . Frequent showers again fell today. . . . Several Indians . . . came into camp. . . . One tree near the tents . . . had been hollowed out to the height of probably eighty feet, and the smoke was even yet escaping from a hole in the side.

Unfortunately, by suppressing fire, much of the region's grasslands and forests have suffered. Many plant species, including the California giant sequoia, need fire; fire helps to clear out some of the heavy canopy that inhibits the growth of seedlings below, while other plant species need fire to help them germinate. And although coastal redwoods dominate in a mixed forest ecosystem, often the tiny seeds of a redwood cannot permeate the thick layers of fallen branches or decaying ferns. Moreover, there is a fungus that can attack the young and fresh roots of a redwood seedling. When a surface fire moves through the forest, it consumes the dry material, sterilizes the soil where the fungus resides, and provides organic matter to induce the seedlings to germinate and grow.

Even Joaquin Miller voiced his concern over the general lack of understanding regarding fire and its ability to preserve, not destroy, the state's most beautiful commodity: trees. The conservation of trees became one of his most important causes. According to Jacqueline Proctor, author of "The Father of Tree Planting in California (aboout Adolph Sutro)":

The poet Joaquin Miller urged the establishment of an Arbor Day celebration in California in 1886 which involved Adolph Sutro and the San Francisco Presidio in 'a vigorous campaign to arouse interest in planting trees on the barren hills surrounding San Francisco Bay.'

Moreover, she noted, "Joaquin Miller planted eucalyptus and other tree species on his 425-acre property in Oakland which was given to the City as a gift by the poet's widow in 1913."

In all, Miller planted about twenty thousand trees on his property in Lake County—in addition to preserving at least one hundred redwood trees. In his conservation efforts, he also noted the role of fire and its impact on the land and landscape.

He wrote occasionally for the *San Francisco Call*. In December 1904, he penned: "The plain truth is there can be no great fires if you have small ones. I do not know that there are advocates of Indian methods. I should say it is mostly a matter of carelessness or indifference. . . . As for the burning up of small trees one should know that nature is most generous here. A thousand little trees are parted to [expose] one that is perfect. . . . Big trees, like big men, must grow wide apart—the survival of the fittest—or tightest."

Joaquin Miller was a strong voice for conservation and preservation of wildlife and nature.

Fire actually burns at three levels, or intensities. Ground fires burn gently, through soil that is rich in organic matter, and return nutrients to the soil. Surface fires burn through accumulated dry matter, which improves the quality of underlying plant growth. Crown fires burn with more heat, traveling up the trees to the canopy above.

Surface fires are generally mild to moderate in scope and can help control the growth of invasive species and groundcover. Crown fires, which can be more devastating, are higher intensity. Fire-management teams are most focused on employing surface fires—which are more "manageable" and far less destructive. Unfortunately, many wildfires—particularly those witnessed in the last few years in the West—have become quite intense, owing in part to drought but also to the level of accumulated dry matter in the forests, woodlands, and grasslands. According to Peter M. Brown in his study of fire in the redwoods, "Increases in fuel loads, tree density, canopy coverage, and formation of ladder fuels result in feedbacks to the fire regime, with the result that crown fires replace surface fires as the dominant fire behavior when fires occur" (rmtrr.org/data/Brown_2007_PSW_GTR-194.pdf).

The tragedy is, ironically, that the years of fire repression have left the forests and prairie lands vulnerable to wildfires that leave little in their wake. Many foresters and logging companies see this as reason enough to allow managed logging. The discussion about the appropriate use and timing of logging and/or salvage logging is an ongoing one.

Notes Steve Norman, "When a forest burns frequently and thus has less plant litter build-up, below-ground soil temperatures rise only slightly and will not be lethal to roots that lie deep in the soil. Although other characteristics of a forest will influence the impact of fire upon it, factors such as climate and topography play an important role in determining fire severity and fire extent. Fires spread most widely during drought years, are most severe on upper slopes and are influenced by the type of vegetation that is growing."

In recent years, Redwood National and State Parks personnel have been using fire in the upland prairies for habitat rejuvenation and to combat invasive species and accumulated fuel loads. One benefit is that the local tribes have increased access to materials used in basketry. Another is that beetles and invasive species can be controlled without the use of pesticides and herbicides.

The story of fire among the coastal redwoods does not, thankfully, follow the same pattern as other western forests. The foggy, humid environment along the coast is not as fire prone. Lightning strikes, which ignite many forest fires, are relatively rare here; in the redwood forests

The Canoe Fire: A Case Study

In 2003 fire erupted in Humboldt Redwoods State Park. Dubbed the Canoe Fire, it burned over eleven thousand acres of old growth and second-growth coast redwood forest. It is considered the most significant coast redwood fire to have burned in the last fifty years, in part due to its extent and in part because of the diversity of vegetation consumed. Perhaps more importantly, the Canoe Fire is significant because it was the first major fire to burn in a protected area since the large-scale acquisition of forestlands and since fire-suppression efforts were initiated in the 1930s.

The fire raised a lot of questions about effective management. Burned were old growth and second-growth redwood forests, as well as upstream riparian areas, mixed-evergreen slopes, former prairies invaded by Douglas fir, and prairies overrun with invasive grasses. The lightning storm that ignited the Canoe Fire on September 3, 2003, kindled at least 273 other fires from San Francisco Bay to the Oregon border. And the fires continued into October.

The actual site where lightning struck was hard to identify because it hit in a remote, rugged part of a wilderness area. In addition, first responders had so many other fires to deal with that the Canoe Fire had ample time to spread to areas where suppression was not possible.

Eventually containment lines were drawn along the watershed boundaries of Canoe Creek and the South Fork of the Eel River, but ultimately the fire burned from the beginning of September until the first week of October and scorched more than ten thousand acres. Because of accepted fire-suppression policies, debris and dry matter on the alluvial terraces had been accumulating since the great flood of 1964, when several feet of sediment was deposited.

people start most fires: whether through carelessness or intention is not always clear. But fire is still an important ingredient in a healthy redwood forest.

Restoration ecology, however, is the approach being practiced by park managers, and controlled burning is a tool that may help restore various environments. The question is, of course, how and when to use fire.

Even a year after the fire, a layer of burned debris reached a depth of one to two centimeters, most from scorched needles that fell during the fire or over the following winter. Following the Canoe Fire, a study was conducted on various cross-sections from trees that were felled during the event in the hopes of determining past fire events. One surprising conclusion: Canoe Creek's alluvial terraces had burned surprisingly often and with similar frequency to dryer upland sites.

More fact-finding revealed that between 1700 and 1850, when the original Sinkyone-Lolangkok people inhabited the area, fires had occurred every ten to fifteen years, and occasionally two or three times in a decade. Even into the 1800s, after the arrival of Euro-Americans, and up until the 1930s, there had been a number of fires.

Understanding the cultural value of fire, most of those fires were likely started by people, whereas lightning started the Canoe Fire. Either way, however, according to the Coast Redwood and Ecology Management website, it was made clear that "regardless of fire history methodologies, . . . the abundance of recorded fire evidence in coast redwood forests clearly indicates that fire had been important. . . . Continued development of protected residual old growth forest and cutover redwood parklands in California toward an appearance of pre-existing conditions may, therefore, be dependent on a fire regime where prescribed burning substitutes for lightning and now-absent aboriginal ignitions."—Mark Finney and Bob Martin, 1989

In addition, "recent assessments of historical fire regimes in coast redwood forests . . . have, for the most part, underestimated the frequency and probable role of surface fires in at least some coast redwood forests over the past several centuries."—Peter Brown and William Baxter, 2003

Wildfire can devastate forests, especially if there has been a significant amount of repressed fire beforehand.
JASHA REYNOLDS, PHOTOGRAPHER. COURTESY JASHA REYNOLDS

In some ways, allowing fire to be a tool is just one means of protecting the environment, and while there is always the potential to damage or destroy the environment, especially in dry prairie lands or in marginal areas, without fire the threat to a healthy system also increases dramatically.

This renewed/revised federal outlook on fire is, in fact, the sum total of a documented and improved understanding of the ecology of forests, prairie lands, and other types of environment. Clearly, many ecosystems—including the coast redwoods—need fire, even depend on it, for rejuvenation or repopulation.

As noted in the USFS website regarding fire, "In recent decades, Redwood National and State Park managers have restored fire in upland prairies in part to provide tribal members with the traditional materials used in basketry and to check the encroachment of Douglas fir. However, the value of adopting a historically-based burning model in residual old growth and second growth is a more difficult question. Fire in redwood can be difficult to control and has both desirable and undesirable consequences—both of which can last for decades to centuries. From the dryer forests of Del Norte County in the north to the southernmost extent of redwood, a modified Native American burning model could easily provide long-term benefit for sustaining and restoring certain desirable forest attributes, particularly in those stands that are at high risk of wildfire" (redwood.forestthreats.org/native.htm).

Looking into the Future:
Restoration and Rehabilitation

Nature, like a loving mother, is ever trying to keep land and sea, mountain and valley, each in its place, to hush the angry winds and waves, balance the extremes of heat and cold, of rain and drought, that peace, harmony, and beauty may reign supreme.
— ELIZABETH CADY STANTON, AUTHOR/SUFFRAGIST,
1815–1902

AS NOTED IN MARK DAVID SPENCE'S 2011 "ADMINISTRATIVE HISTORY" report, "The struggle to craft a Master Plan for RNP neatly demonstrates the full range of challenges that faced park managers through the mid-1970s—and largely confirms the assessment that conditions were indeed 'impossible.'" After a special study was conducted in 1968, it was concluded that "the Park Service should let out the assignment [i.e.: how best to protect the park's newly established boundaries], to an academic researcher . . . by the year's end, the NPS contracted with Edward C. Stone at the University of California's School of Forestry in Berkeley to craft a 'management prescription for lands surrounding the Park that would minimize any deleterious effects they might have on park resources.'" Stone's report became the basis for planning. Unfortunately, the report—completed in haste—was rejected by the Sierra Club and other environmental groups, which argued that the Park Service was placing too much emphasis on practices outside the park versus protecting the park itself. The draft master plan, released in 1971, was submitted to the Secretary of the Interior in 1973.

However, after Congress passed NEPA (National Environmental Policy Act)—which required agencies to submit statements on significant actions—it became clear that the Park Service had not developed a procedure for compliance, making the Master Plan unwieldy and unworkable. In spite of this, park officials accomplished much, including construction or improvement in facilities, development of interpretive programming, drafting agreements with private landowners as well as state and federal agencies, and pulling together important historical, archaeological, and natural resources "inventories."

As the park opened to its first visitors in 1969, RNP's personnel included only six permanent employees, and the budget for operations was $82,000. The headquarters was located in a rented space in Crescent City, while a portable trailer was set up in Orick. The old Yurok Redwood Experimental Forest Administration building in Klamath provided space for seasonal workers.

Between 1970 and 1974, however, there was a yearly increase of 30 percent in visitations, and more than 328,000 tourists came through the park in 1975.

The focus of RNP rangers and officials soon became that of "rehabilitation," a term that had two meanings. On the one hand, it referred to the restoration of old structures and facilities for park use; on the other hand, it also applied to the occasional duties of some work crews to take part in a "continuing project to rehabilitate cut-over lands in the Park" that, by 1975, included "restoring natural drainages to up to four miles of road annually."

Again, according to Mark David Spence, "The years after expansion were about more than just following the will of Congress and implementing legislated programs. . . . Even as Redwood [National Park] embarked on what Superintendent Robert Barbee called 'the beginning of a new era,' the old and inherent necessity of adapting to changing conditions within the park and outside its boundaries remained the guiding principle of park management." He added, "In short, successfully administering the extended park meant actively engaging the dynamic ecological, political, and social conditions in which it was situated."

From this point forward, "most Natural Resource Management projects operated within, or in support of, the watershed rehabilitation program." This included fish studies and assessment of spawning sites and rearing areas and the overall health of potential salmon habitat. In addition, wildlife management programs were implemented, including the park's Roosevelt elk and black bear (*Ursus americanus*) management plans.

In fact, "RNP's resource management program—apart from watershed rehabilitation—became an influential player beyond the park and the Park Service. In 1989 and 1990, park staff became involved in the formation of the California Regional Strategy to Conserve Biological Diversity."

Another link in the chain of development of Redwood National and State Parks was the consolidation of RNP and the three state parks originally destined to become a part of the larger entity. Following the 1990 election of Governor Pete Wilson, efforts to resolve the overlooked and/or neglected subject of consolidation came to the forefront. Many hoped the oversight had been a bureaucratic issue, but the matter would prove more complicated.

According to Mark David Spence's report, "The issues ranged from concerns about losing the 'crown jewels' of the state park system to a sense that NPS regulations would be more restrictive than state park rules regarding issues like beach access, camping, driftwood gathering, and beach fires." Some also worried that personnel within the state system might suffer a setback when it came to salaries, benefits, seniority, and promotions. Eventually it became clear that a cooperative management agreement between NPS and the California Department of Parks and Recreation (CDPR) was the right path to take. In January 1994, a draft report recommended that an "operational memorandum of understanding (MOU) between the CDPR and NPS [be adopted] and recommended that the federal and state park lands be known collectively as the Redwood National and State Parks." As a result, the park established another important precedent regarding land management, and in 1995, the National Park Foundation awarded the superintendents of RNSP the National Park Partnership Leadership Award for Resource Stewardship and Preservation, "in recognition of their innovative partnership . . . in developing joint management strategies for the adjoining redwood parks along the North Coast."

Such is the history of this unique and important park. As noted in the Redwood General Management Plan, drafted in 1998, the purpose for creating this national park was to "preserve significant examples of the primeval coastal redwood forests and the prairies, streams, seashores, and woodlands with which they are associated in a condition of unimpaired ecological integrity, for the purposes of public inspiration, enjoyment, and scientific study, and to preserve all related scenic, historic, and recreational values. The park was then expanded 'with particular attention to minimizing siltation of the streams' and 'in order to protect existing irreplaceable Redwood National Park resources from damaging upslope and upstream land uses.'"

Watershed restoration and rehabilitation have resulted in critical improvements and restored habitat for the redwoods and surrounding landscape, as well as for the multiple species of plants and animals that abide there.

In truth, any parklands or protected lands provide opportunities for people to escape, relax, and reconnect with nature and the world in general. On a practical level, they also improve local economies. According to studies conducted by the Centers for Disease Control and Prevention, creating or providing places like parks encourages people to be more physically active and improves individual and community health. Protected public lands also help improve water quality, protect groundwater, prevent flooding, improve the quality of the air we breathe, provide vegetative buffers to development, produce and protect habitat for wildlife, and provide a place for families to connect with nature or recreate outdoors together.

In addition, a study by the Trust for Public Land shows that in the past ten years, voter approval for bond measures that provide money for conserving open space or establishing parks exceeded 75 percent. Finally, public parks add value to a community or region that transcends the money invested or revenues gained from fees.

Organizations such as the Sierra Club, the Sempervirens Fund, and the Save-the-Redwoods League, among others, likewise serve the public by supporting and providing donations and funds for the purchase of private lands. Since 1918, for example, the Save-the-Redwoods League has raised over $31 million and has established more than a thousand memorial groves in thirty of California's redwood parks; with corresponding matching funds, 189,000 acres of ancient redwood forestland have been protected.

The League continues to conduct research, offers education about the redwoods, and initiates fund-raising campaigns to help buy more forestland. Over the last ten years, it has also awarded more than twenty-five research grants to scientists. Its purpose, as outlined on its website, states:

> *We protect redwoods by purchasing redwood forests and the surrounding lands needed to nurture them. Another way we protect forests is by acquiring conservation easements or agreements, which grant the League the legal right to safeguard the forest from harmful land use practices forever. Our science-based Master Plan for the Redwoods guides our efforts to protect and restore redwood forests. This plan identifies where we need to protect land to strengthen the forests we have conserved since our founding in 1918. The Master Plan incorporates the theory and principles of conservation biology. These principles guide Save-the-Redwoods to protect large blocks of contiguous redwood land that embrace the diversity of the forest.*

Another multi-agency project undertaken with the League was the purchase of the Mill and Rock Creek watersheds, completed in 2002. The 25,000-acre property, added to Del Norte Coast Redwoods State Park, borders Jedediah Smith Redwoods State Park to the north and Six Rivers National Forest to the east and connected Jedediah Smith Redwoods State Park to Redwood National Park.

Because the Mill Creek Watershed supports a significant run of coho salmon within the Smith River watershed, it is considered critical to the species' continued recovery. Thus the Mill Creek Watershed Addition of 2002 provided an opportunity to begin important restoration. From 1954 until 2000, it had been managed intensively for timber production, and a network of logging roads and trails traversed the area, leaving the region subject to erosion, negatively impacting the watershed.

Another project that involved the Save-the-Redwoods League and the InterTribal Sinkyone Wilderness Council (a nonprofit consortium of ten federally recognized northern California Indian tribes) was the donation of Four Corners to the council.

Four Corners is located a few hours north of San Francisco in northern Mendocino County, at the four corners of Briceland-Whitethorn Road and Usal Road. It's a 164-acre parcel covered with beautiful redwoods and once served as a special meeting place for native peoples. As part of the agreement, the council granted the League a conservation easement, protecting the property from future development and natural resource extraction.

"Our agreement with the Council will ensure the land essentially remains in its current state by precluding commercial harvesting and further development," said Ruskin K. Hartley, former executive director of the Save-the-Redwoods League. "It also includes provisions that allow a critical trail corridor to be built that will connect portions of Sinkyone Wilderness State Park along the Mattole River with those at the coast."

Other projects on tap include a project to purchase the Big River–Mendocino Old-Growth Redwoods, located about one mile from the Pacific Ocean and Mendocino, where two rare forest types exist, including a pygmy forest and an ancient redwood forest; a $10 million project with the California Wildlife Conservation Board to help protect San Vicente Redwoods and the Santa Cruz Mountains' ecosystem; a project to restore an easy-access gateway to Peters Creek Old-Growth Forest in the Santa Cruz Mountains; and a project between Sequoia Riverlands Trust and the Bureau of Land Management.

In recognition of Save-the-Redwoods' purchase of the candelabra redwoods and the Shady Dell tract, the Redwood Forest Foundation dedicated a "Founder's Tree" in its honor in 2013. This highest honor was given the League and four other organizations and individuals who "played an absolutely crucial and fundamental role in helping the Foundation to achieve its important mission of acquiring and conserving California's redwood forests." The other honorees were the Conservation Fund, Wildlife Conservation Board, State Coastal Conservancy, and Donald S. Kemp, PhD, and Edgar B. Kemp Jr. The five Founder's Trees are located in the Usal Redwood Forest, near the old town of Kenny (which had its last post office in 1924).

Another organization to provide support is the National Parks Conservation Association. Established in 1919, its membership has reached 340,000, with twenty-five regional offices. In 2000 the association initiated the State of the Parks Program, which assesses conditions within various parks; it also studies the park's stewardship. The goal is "to provide information that will help policymakers, the public, and the National Park Service improve conditions in national parks, celebrate successes as models for other parks, and ensure a lasting legacy for future generations."

Redwood Forest Foundation, Inc. (RFFI), a nonprofit organization, was formed in 1997. Uniquely, the board of directors includes representation from the timber industry, local activist groups, the banking community, and educators. The goal: to create a new partnership and ownership model, through county-based advisory committees who serve as "shareholders" in the corporation's decision-making process.

In June 2007 the Redwood Forest Foundation purchased almost 51,000 acres of coastal redwoods in northwestern Mendocino County with $65 million borrowed from Bank of America. The tract stretches from the Pacific Ocean to the Eel River along US Highway 101.

According to Art Harwood, president of RFFI, "This [purchase] is the beginning of a new era for our local community. We are banding together to protect and manage our forests. We are pulling together private capital, and the hopes and aspirations of people from all walks of life to create a bright beacon for our future. We are doing this by ending the 30 years of fighting, and focusing on what unites us."

According to a document prepared by Jason R. Teroaka, titled *Forest Restoration at Redwood National Park: A Case Study of an Emerging Program*:

> *For more than 30 years Redwood National Park has been working to establish a Forest Restoration Program to rehabilitate its impaired, second growth forests. This case study outlines the Park's history of using silviculture as a restoration tool, which began in 1978 after the Park's expansion. The most recent effort was the 1,700-acre South Fork of Lost Man Creek Forest Restoration Project where two silvicultural prescriptions were used. Low thinning on ridge top sites reduced basal area by 40 percent, and wood generated was sold as forest products. Crown thinning on steep mid slope sites reduced basal area by 25 percent, and the wood was lopped and scattered. Permanent plots were established before thinning and were reassessed after thinning.*

The park established a two-hundred-acre experimental thinning effort referred to as the Holter Ridge Thinning Study. The area had been clear-cut in 1954 and was dominated by Douglas fir.

Again, according to Teroaka, "This marked the first time that trees were cut down at Redwood National Park as a restoration effort. National Park Service executives, however, disagreed with the notion that thinning could be used as a restoration tool; others expressed frustration that the Park was cutting down trees on land removed from timber production. Finally, a moratorium on thinning second growth forests in the Park was established in 1979, and the Park's first attempt at forest restoration came to an end."

Watershed restoration has become the key to reestablishing a balanced environment within the Redwood National and State Parks. With the expansion of the park in 1978, the goal became one of establishing and protecting watersheds as well as preserving remaining old growth redwoods along the creeks and waterways.

Studies identified old logging roads as the leading cause of erosion. Again, according to the National Park Service, "Standards for logging methods and road construction did not exist prior to enactment of the California Forest Practice Act of 1973. . . . Many had inadequate drainage structures, such as culverts sized too small to carry heavy winter flows; roads washed out and triggered severe gully and landslide erosion. The skid roads that bulldozers used to drag logs from hillsides to roads became the new drainage network."

As a result, the Redwood Creek watershed was seriously affected and altered by the silt and erosion left behind as a result of past environmental impacts, particularly floods or landslides, and old logging practices. After a series of projects that failed to reestablish timber on the gullied slopes, park personnel decided that to restore the watershed and correct the problem—i.e., abandoned logging roads—they would have to reemploy the same equipment that "built" the problem.

Bulldozers and excavators were used to remove old culverts and re-expose original streambeds. Uncovered tree stumps became the clues to the original slope of the land. Woody debris was scattered over recovered surfaces to reduce the potential erosion, while organic matter was added to the soil. In time, even within a few months, native forest species began to reestablish themselves.

As noted again in the Watershed Restoration project literature, "Restoring nature's landscape design brings back natural hillslope and stream channel processes. Re-exposed topsoil is rich in nutrients, organic matter, and native seed. In a few years, road removal effects begin to fade from view as trees take root in a natural setting."

To assist with the restoration, local timber contractors and tribal members, as well as heavy equipment operators, were hired to help remove 450 miles of logging and 3,500 miles of skid roads. In fact, over $103 million was paid out to more than 2,850 timber workers in the years following the 1987 acquisition.

Geologist Terry Spreiter expressed the park's point of view: "The best roads are those that no one, including Mother Nature, knows were ever there."

With the 1990s and the controversial listing of the spotted owl as an endangered species came the development of the Northwest Forest Plan, which proposed that goals include maintaining a healthy ecosystem while providing for a continued, reasonable timber harvest. The plan also called for more restoration efforts, including thinning as a way to regenerate the forests. However, when a logging company proposed cutting five hundred acres of old growth redwoods, because the marbled murrelet had also been listed as an endangered species, a local environmental group challenged the plan in court. Mitigation dollars that the lumber company had offered to provide the park for its thinning project were stopped. As a result, the Forest Restoration Plan was scrapped.

According to Teroaka, "In 1999, the Parks' General Management Plan was approved, and provided the compliance needed to revive the Forest Restoration Program. To build momentum for the program, a park-wide forest inventory was conducted to describe the range of resource conditions and to use the data to prioritize areas for treatment. . . . Based on the assessment of the Park's second growth forests, the South Fork of Lost Man Creek drainage was chosen as the first major forest restoration project." The plan was approved in 2009; its objectives were to reduce forest density to promote redwood composition, while promoting understory vegetation and vigorous tree growth.

The result? "The thinning increased redwood composition relative to Douglas-fir. Prior to thinning, there were 32.2 percent more Douglas-fir than redwood and Douglas-fir had 40.3 percent more basal area than redwood. Immediately after thinning, there were 191.3 percent more redwood than Douglas-fir and redwood had 80.2 percent more basal area than Douglas-fir."

As noted by G. F. Beranek:

The California Forest Practice Act was amended in 1973 to contain a provision that timber harvest plans for commercial operations be prepared by Registered Professional Foresters. It was the beginning of a revolution in Forest Practice and Range Management in California, and since then THPs (Timber Harvest Plans) have grown from a few pages into volumes. Plus the THP grew from a mere description into a prescription that takes into consideration many things not even considered before. Stocking requirements, heritage and leave trees, watercourse and lake protection zones, landscape stability, slope exclusion,

*road building requirements and restrictions, sensitive watershed and
the Endangered Species Act. . . . It's come a long way in 30 years.*

Now, thirty-plus years later, governmental and regulatory agencies,
as well as the environmental community and conservation organizations,
have accepted the idea that thinning young forests and applying the use
of appropriate fire can improve an ecosystem's value. Most importantly,
there is a long-term and continued effort to understand the nature and
world of the redwoods. Outside and inside the boundaries of the Redwood National and State Parks system, just how to preserve the magnificent stands of ancient tall trees has become a national passion.

Propagation of redwoods has occurred in a variety of ways over the
years. Countries outside the United States have attempted to establish
plantations, such as in New Zealand, but for the most part, they remain
ornamental or experimental. Coast redwoods have been propagated in
Japan and China, as well as in Mexico, Europe, and on the Hawaiian
islands of Maui, Kauai, and Oahu. Some of those trees have grown to
be more than a hundred feet tall. One coast redwood over 130 years
old can be found on Isola Madre in Lake Maggiore in northern Italy.
Much of France is too cold for the coast redwood's survival, although
giant sequoias have fared far better there. Sierra giants seem to prosper
in Germany as well.

On the east coast of the United States, the oldest and largest coast
redwood can be found in Norfolk, Virginia; reportedly a Captain Weir,
who brought redwood seedlings around Cape Horn from California,
planted it in 1850. Only one tree survived; today the tree stands over a
hundred feet tall.

The diversity that exists in Redwood National and State Parks is part
of its allure. From steep mountainsides timbered with tall trees, down to
the rugged coastline and stretches of sand and broad or narrow lagoons,
across prairies and grasslands and back into the hills and river canyons,
the experience is unique and inspiring. There is nothing like California's
tall trees or redwood country.

It isn't enough to preserve just sections of redwoods or particular
groves; it's imperative that the entire system surrounding the redwood

region be understood and protected and/or rehabilitated. Redwoods are vulnerable and their ecosystem is a complex one that demands a more holistic and comprehensive approach to preservation.

For so many reasons, the history behind the creation of the Redwood National and State Parks has been a complex one—with controversies that pitted communities and organizations against one another. Dramas had to be played out in Congress, in court, and between individuals, but the end result is captured in the massive and preserved groves of the world's tallest and most unique trees.

There are a multitude of reasons why Redwood National and State Parks are so important to California, the nation, the world: 1) the parks preserve the largest contiguous region of ancient coast redwood forest, including some of its tallest and oldest trees; 2) the region is now the subject of restoration programs designed to recover the area's original or "lost values"; 3) the region rests near the junction of three active tectonic plates and frequent earthquakes, which influence the geography and nat-ural characteristics of the park; 4) the parks contain a "mosaic" of habitats that are home to a number of rare or endangered species; 5) the parks encompass approximately thirty-five miles of coastline and related rivers, including portions of the Redwood Creek, Klamath River, and Smith River watersheds; 6) the parks' region is tied to the history and culture of four California tribes, including the Tolowa, Yurok, Chilula, and Hupa; 7) the region also represents the history of 150 years of non-Native land use and settlement; and 8) the region is recognized as a United Nations World Heritage site. International Biosphere Reserve Status was granted in the 1980s.

Truly, for those who make a living in the forest, trees mean life. For those who find refuge in the forest, the trees that shelter them provide the breath of fresh life. No matter what point of view anyone takes as they walk through California's magnificent redwoods, it is hard not to feel the spirit of these ancient wonders.

Their future—and our future—depends on how we care for them. Employing good management, whether through preservation and pro-tection or balanced by managed logging, prescribed fire, thinning, or propagating, the future of the redwoods depends on all of us.

In the words of John Muir, "It has been said that trees are imperfect men, and seem to bemoan their imprisonment rooted in the ground. But they never seem so to me. I never saw a discontented tree. They grip the ground as though they liked it and though fast rooted they travel about as far as we do. They go wandering forth in all directions with every wind, going and coming like ourselves, traveling with us around the sun two million miles a day, and through space heaven knows how fast and far!"

BIBLIOGRAPHY

Alden, Peter, et al. *National Audubon Society Field Guide to California*. New York: Alfred A. Knopf, 2005.

Arvola, T. F. *Regulation of Logging in California: 1945–1975*. Sacramento: State of California Department of Conservation, Division of Forestry, 1976.

Bearss, Edwin C. *Redwood National Park: History/Basic Data. Del Norte and Humboldt Counties, California*. Division of History, Office of Archeology and Historic Preservation, US Department of the Interior, 1969.

Beranek, Gerald F. *High Climbers and Timber Fallers*. Ft. Bragg, CA: Beranek Publications, 2005.

Betts, John and Daniel G. Foster et al, *History of the California Department of Forestry and Fire Protection Archaeology Program, 1970-2004*. State Department of Forestry and Fire Protection, 2004.

Brown, Peter M. "What Was the Role of Fire in Coast Redwood Forests?" rmtrr.org/data/Brown_2007_PSW_GTR-194.pdf.

Brown, Peter M. and W. T. Baxter. "Fire History in Coast Redwood Forests of the Coast Mendocino Coast, California." research.wsulibs.wsu.edu:8443/xmlui/handle/2376/806.

Brown, Vinson. *Native Americans of the Pacific Coast: Peoples of the Sea Wind*. Happy Camp, CA: Naturgraph, 1977/1985.

California Digital Newspaper Collection. cdnc.ucr.edu/cgi-bin/cdnc?a=d&d=SFC19080223.2.11&srpos=29&e=-------en--20-SFC-21--txt-txIN-redwood+preservation------#.

Carranco, Lynwood, and John T. Labbe. *Logging the Redwoods*. Caldwell, ID: Caxton Press, 2010.

Carranco, Lynwood, and Henry L. Sorensen. *Steam in the Redwoods*. Caldwell, ID: Caxton Printers, 1988.

"Changing Perceptions of Fire in Coast Redwood Forests." Coast Redwood Ecology and Management. redwood.forestthreats.org/perceptions.htm.

Clar, C. Raymond. *California Government and Forestry: from Spanish Days until the creation of the Department of Natural Resources in 1927*. Sacramento: Division of Forestry, Department of Natural Resources, State of California. 1959.

Coast Redwood Ecology and Management. redwood.forestthreats.org/index.html.

Crump, Spencer. *Redwoods, Iron Horses and The Pacific: The Story of the California Western Skunk Railroad*. Los Angeles: Trans-Anglo Books, 1963/1965.

Dickinson, A. Bray, with Roy Graves, Ted Wurm, and Al Graves. *Narrow Gauge to the Redwoods: The Story of the North Pacific Coast Railroad and San Francisco Bay Paddle-wheel Ferries.* Glendale, CA: Trans-Anglo Books, 1981.

Discover the Redwoods. http://discovertheredwoods.com/history-highway-101 -through-redwoods. 2011-2015.

"Ecosystem Restoration and Management." National Park Service. nature.nps.gov/ biology/ecosystemrestoration/index.cfm.

"Fires Were Common in Rainy Northern Forests." Save-the-Redwoods League. savetheredwoods.org/grant/fires-were-common-in-rainy-northern-forests/.

Frome, Michael, and David Muench. *Western National Parks.* Chicago: Rand McNally & Company, 1977.

Gibbs, George. "Excerpts from the Journal of Reddick McKee Expedition." *Siskiyou Pioneer and Yearbook 2, no. 3* (Spring 1953). Yreka, CA: Siskiyou County Historical Society.

"The Gold Rush Eased into the Settlement Era." *Arcata Eye,* July 24, 2013. arcataeye .com/2013/07/the-gold-rush-eased-into-the-settlement-era.

Goddard, Pliny Earle. *Notes on the Chilula Indians of Northwestern California.* Berkeley: University of California Press, 1914.

Graves, Charles S. *Before the White Man Came.* Yreka, CA: Siskiyou News, 1934.

"The Great Quake, 1906–2006 / Earthquake Diary: Helen Wild." *SFGate,* April 9, 2006. sfgate.com/news/article/The-Great-Quake-1906-2006-Earthquake -diary-2499985.php.

Harris, David. *The Last Stand: The War Between Wall Street and Main Street Over California's Ancient Redwoods.* San Francisco: Sierra Club Books, 1996.

Hawk, Diane. *Touring the Old Redwood Highway: Del Norte County.* Piercy, CA: Hawk Mountaintop Publishing, 2006.

Hewes, Jeremy Joan. *Redwoods: The World's Largest Trees.* Chicago: Rand McNally & Company, 1981.

"History of Highway 101 Through the Redwoods." Discover the Redwoods. discovertheredwoods.com/history-highway-101-through-redwoods.

"Historic California Posts, Camps, Stations and Airfields: Fort Ross (Fort Rossiya)." militarymuseum.org/FtRoss.html.

Home of the Redwood: A Souvenir of the Lumber Industry of California. San Francisco: S. L. Everett, Publisher, 1897.

"Humboldt California's Redwood Coast: Explore Redwood National Park." redwoods .info/showrecord.asp?id=475&source=Favorites.

Hyde, Leslie Daggett. "Indian Legends." *Siskiyou Pioneer and Yearbook 2, no. 3* (Spring 1953). Yreka, CA: Siskiyou County Historical Society.

Hyde, Philip, and Francois Leydet. *The Last Redwoods.* San Francisco: Sierra Club, 1963.

Johnston, Hank. *They Felled the Redwoods.* Los Angeles: Trans-Anglo Books, 1966.

Kellogg, Mike. Personal interview, July 11, 2015.

"Kent Is Guest of Native Sons." *San Francisco Call,* February 23, 1908. cdnc.ucr.edu/cgi -bin/cdnc?a=d&d=SFC19080223.2.11&srpos=29&e=-------en--20-SFC-21 --txt-txIN-redwood+preservation------#.

Kneiss, Gilbert H. *Redwood Railways: A Story of Redwoods, Picnics and Commuters.* Berkeley, CA: Howell-North, 1956.

Kroeber, Alfred L. *Yurok Myths.* Berkeley: University of California Press, 1978.

Lake, Robert G. *Chilula: People from the Ancient Redwoods.* Lanham, MD: University Press of America, 1982.

Leydet, François. *The Last Redwoods and the Parkland of Redwood Creek.* New York: Sierra Club/Ballantine Books, 1969.

Mark, Stephen R. *Preserving the Living Past: John C. Merriam's Legacy in the State and National Parks.* Berkeley: University of California Press, 2005.

Masson, Marcelle. "By-paths of the Wintu." *Siskiyou Pioneer and Yearbook, Vol. 2, No. 3* (Spring 1953). Yreka, CA: Siskiyou County Historical Society.

McClurkan, Carolyn S. *Redwood National Park Establishment Papers.* Crescent City, CA: National Park Service, 1999.

McConnell, Robert. Personal interview, July 13, 2015.

McDowell, Jack, ed. *A Sunset Pictorial: Discovering the California Coast.* Menlo Park, CA: Lane Publishing, 1975/1978.

Mendocino Redwood Company, LLC. mrc.com/.

Merriam, John C. *A Living Link in History.* Berkeley, CA: Save-the-Redwoods League, 1930.

Miller, Joaquin. "Plea for Forest Fire Prevention." *San Francisco Morning Call.* (28 December 1904): 11: 28.

Morgan, Dale L. *Jedediah Smith and the Opening of the West.* Lincoln: University of Nebraska Press, 1953.

Morley, James M. *Muir Woods: The Ancient Redwood Forest Near San Francisco.* San Francisco: Smith-Morley, 1991.

Muir, John. *Northwest Passages: From the Pen of John Muir in California, Oregon, Washington, and Alaska.* Wellsboro, PA: Tioga Publishing Company, 1988.

Nixon, Stuart. *Redwood Empire: An Illustrated History of the California Redwood Country.* New York: Galahad Books, 1966.

Norton, Jack. *Genocide in Northwestern California: When Our Worlds Cried.* San Francisco: The Indian Historian Press, Inc., 1979.

Palmer, Rose Amelia. *The North American Indians: An Account of the American Indians North of Mexico.* New York: Smithsonian Institution, Inc. Series, Volume 4, 1929.

Pararas-Carayannis, Dr. George. "California Tsunami: The March 28, 1964 Tsunami in California." drgeorgepc.com/Tsunami1964Calif.html.

Pararas-Carayannis, George. "The Effects of the March 27, 1964 Alaska Tsunami in California." Disaster Pages of Dr. George Pararas-Carayannis. drgeorgepc.com/Tsunami1964Calif.html

Proctor, Jacqueline. "The Father of Tree Planting in California." mtdavidson.org/the-father-of-tree-planting-in-california. 2014.

Purslow, Neil. *Natural Wonders: Redwood National Park Forest of Giants.* New York: Weigl Publishers, 2007.

Raphael, Ray, and Freeman House. *Two Peoples, One Place: Humboldt History, Vol. 1.* Arcata, CA: Creative Type Productions, 2007/2011.

"Redwood Ecotours: Native Americans." redwoodecotours.com/native-american.htm.

Redwood National and State Parks. nps.gov/redw/index.htm. 2015.

Redwood National and State Parks Humboldt and Del Norte Counties: Draft General Management Plan/General Plan. National Park Service: US Department of the Interior, June 1998.

Redwood National and State Parks: Watershed Restoration. National Park Service: US Department of the Interior, 1999.

Rohde, Jerry, and Gisela Rohde. *Redwood National and State Parks: Tales, Trails, and Auto Tours.* McKinleyville, CA: MountainHome Books, 1994.

Samoa Cookhouse Historic Logging Museum. samoacookhouse.net/samoa-cookhouse -museum.html.

Schrader, George R. "Karoc Ceremonials." *Siskiyou Pioneer and Yearbook 2*, no. 3 (Spring 1953). Yreka, CA: Siskiyou County Historical Society.

"Scotia (Forestville)." Timber Heritage Association. timberheritage.org/timber -company-towns/scotia.

Spence, Mark David. *Watershed Park: Administrative History Redwood National and State Parks.* National Park Service. 2011.

Strobridge, William F. *Regulars in the Redwoods: The US Army in Northern California 1852–1861.* Spokane, WA: Arthur H. Clark Company, 1994.

Sudworth, George B. *Forest Trees of the Pacific Slope.* New York: Dover Publications, 1967.

Taylor, Arthur Adelbert. *California Redwood Park, Sometimes called Sempervirens Park; An Appreciation.* Sacramento: W. Richardson, 1912.

Taylor, Bayard. *New Pictures from California.* Oakland: Biobooks, 1951.

Thompson, Lucy (Che-na-wah Weitch-ah-wah). "To the American Indian." Eureka, California, 1916. archive.org/stream/amerindianslucy00thomrich/amerindians lucy00thomrich_djvu.txt.

Tushingham, Shannon. *Publications in Cultural Heritage, No. 30: Archaeology, Ethnography, and Tolowa Heritage at Red Elderberry Place, Chvn-su'lh-dvn, Jedediah Smith Redwoods State Park.* California Department of Parks and Recreation, 2013.

Tweed, William C. *Sequoia–Kings Canyon: The Story Behind the Scenery.* Las Vegas, NV: KC Publications, 1985.

Vaden, Mario D. "Welcome to Coast Redwood Parks." http://www.mdvaden.com/ grove_of_titans.shtml.

———. "Largest Coast Redwoods, Year of Discovery, 2014." mdvaden.com/redwood_ year_discovery.shtml.

Van Dyke, Walter. "Early Days in Klamath." Virtual Museum of the City of San Francisco. sfmuseum.net/hist7/klamath.html.

Van Pelt, Dr. Robert. *Forest Giants of the Pacific Coast.* Seattle: University of Washington Press, 2002.

Waterman, T. T. *Yurok Geography.* Trinidad, CA: Trinidad Museum Society, 1993. First published 1920 by University of California Press.

Wayburn, Edgar. "Sierra Club Statesman, Leader of the Parks and Wilderness Movement: Gaining Protection for Alaska, the Redwoods, and Golden Gate Parklands." Interview conducted by Ann Lage and Susan Schrepfer. Berkeley: Regents of the University of California and the Sierra Club, 1985.

Westfall, Andy. *Humboldt Heartland*. Ferndale, CA: Humboldt Heartland, 2010.

Wheeler, James. Personal interview, July 10, 2015.

White, Mike. *Top Trails: Northern California's Redwood Coast Must-Do Hikes for Everyone*. Birmingham, AL: Wilderness Press, 2014.

Whitney, Stephen. *A Sierra Club Naturalist's Guide to the Pacific Northwest*. San Francisco: Sierra Club Books, 1989.

Yurok Tribe. yuroktribe.org.

Yurok Tribe: Pue-lik-lo', Pey-cheek-lo', Ner-er-ner'. Yurok Tribal Council, 2007.

INDEX

ABOUT THE AUTHOR

Gail L. Fiorini-Jenner has completed two historical novels and four non-fiction titles on regional history, including three books on the mythical State of Jefferson. Her first novel won a WILLA Literary Award from Women Writing the West. She edited and contributed to an anthology, *Ankle High and Knee Deep: Women Reflect on Western Rural Life*, released in 2014, that reached Amazon's Top 100 books on country living in its first thirty days. She writes monthly for a regional publication and has sold numerous articles, children's stories, and women's stories to a variety of publishers and publications. She has appeared on History Channel's *How the States Got Their Shapes*, as well as on *Mysteries at the Museum* and *Legends and Lies*. She also appeared on *Oregon Experience: The State of Jefferson* on Oregon PBS (which won a Spur Award) and writes for Jefferson Public Radio's historical "As It Was" series. Gail is a member of Women Writing the West, Western Writers of America, and Rogue Writers Ink, as well as her local historical society and CattleWomen's Association. As a retired history and English teacher, she volunteers at her local museums and library. She is the wife of a fourth-generation cattle rancher, which contributes to an active, outdoor lifestyle that adds to her love of local and regional history.

Made in the USA
Monee, IL
19 November 2022

18127322R00121